The Afro-Spanish American Author

Garland Reference Library
of the Humanities
(Vol. 194)

The Afro-Spanish American Author
*An Annotated Bibliography
of Criticism*

Richard L. Jackson

Garland Publishing, Inc. • New York & London
1980

Library of Congress Cataloging in Publication Data

Jackson, Richard L   1937–
  The Afro-Spanish American author.

  (Garland reference library of the humanities ;
v. 194)
  Includes index.
  1. Spanish American literature—Black authors—
History and criticism—Bibliography. I. Title.
Z1609.L7J32 [PQ7081]   016.860'8   79-7928
ISBN 0-8240-9529-4

Printed on acid-free, 250-year-life paper
Manufactured in the United States of America

Contents

Acknowledgments

I would like to thank Keith Edghill for his research assistance, the Interlibrary Loan Department of Carleton University for its help in locating material, and Lawrence Davidow for his helpful suggestions. I would also like to thank Mrs. Nicolette Bravo for her usual good typing and for her careful adherence to manuscript specifications. I express as well my gratitude to my wife, Lillian, who has to find time to read everything I write.

Introduction
Trends in Afro-Spanish American Literary Criticism

José Mariátegui, the great Peruvian essayist and defender of the Indian, held the Black in low regard. He did make one statement, however, that can legitimately apply to the black experience in Spanish America. Mariátegui once said, in effect, that authentic Indian literature would come about only when Indians themselves were in a position to produce it.[1] This holds true equally for Blacks and for the emergence of authentic black literature, that is, literature written by Blacks in Spanish America, particularly in this century. Also emerging, as this bibliography illustrates, is a growing body of literary criticism produced by black and nonblack critics both inside and outside of Spanish America. Indeed, as the Afro-Spanish American author has become more visible, the criticism of his works has increased at an unprecedented rate; Afro-Spanish American literary criticism has enjoyed its own kind of boom in recent years.

Some time ago Arturo Torres-Rioseco wrote that "the development of a literary criticism denotes in a certain sense the maturity of a literature."[2] While the "full growth"—as Torres-Rioseco calls it—that comes with the cultivation of mature criticism has not yet been reached, there can be little doubt that Afro-Spanish American literary criticism is one of the fastest maturing disciplines within the field of Hispanic studies. Though

1. *Seven Interpretative Essays on Peruvian Reality* (*Siete ensayos de interpretación de la realidad peruana*) (1928), translated by Marjory Urquidi. Austin: University of Texas Press, 1971, p. 274.

2. *New World Literature. Tradition and Revolt in Latin America.* Berkeley and Los Angeles: University of California Press, 1949, p. 138.

this surge in critical activity is recent, there have for many years been dedicated Hispanists interested in black themes in Spanish American literature, particularly in Cuba in the 1930's and 1940's. We can also point to the earlier example of Francisco Calcagno's *Poetas de color* (1868), one of the first studies in Spanish America to single out black writers as an authentic group worthy of critical recognition.

The present annotated bibliography attempts to further such recognition by limiting its frame of reference to the Afro-Spanish American author. While there are several general bibliographies available (see Section I), this is the only available annotated book-length bibliography that focuses exclusively on the Afro-Spanish American author, his works, and criticism of them. By annotating criticism only where it has some bearing on the Afro-Spanish American as author, I exclude those nonblack authors—and the criticism of them—who have taken the Black as subject and theme. The list of primary creative works of the Afro-Spanish American authors themselves helps to lend cohesive treatment to this specific group of black authors writing in Spanish.

I have prepared this bibliography largely to complement my *Black Writers in Latin America* (see No. 46), which is also designed to focus on the black writer as a group. One of the purposes of that book, and one that is also reflected in this bibliography, is to show that black literature in Latin America is more than simply vernacular literature. Further, although writing as a group within an inherited black literary tradition, black writers in Latin America are at the same time representative of the concerns, styles, and literary movements associated with Latin America as a whole. While black literature in Latin America has its own parallel literary history, this should not detract from the enrichment its presence brings to the larger Latin American literature. To cite a few parallel but integrated examples: Gaspar Octavio Hernández carried the nickname "The Black Swan," but he was also known as Panama's foremost Modernist poet. Arnoldo Palacios' *Las estrellas son negras* is a very "black" book, but it may also be Colombia's outstanding Naturalist novel. Plácido was shot partly because of his color, which made it easier for the authorities to read seditious and racial sentiment into his poetry. But Plácido was to many Cuba's Romantic poet, one who through his *criollo* verse was partly responsible for founding a distinctive Cuban school of poetry as opposed to the Castillian. Adalberto Ortiz's *Juyungo*, Juan Pablo Sojo's *Nochebuena negra*, and Manuel Zapata Olivella's *Chambacú, corral de negros* are "black" novels, but they are also Latin American novels of the selva, of the land, and of the city respectively.

Entries in this bibliography cover these and most of the other major black authors who have published books, and most of the titles indispensable for an awareness of the multiple critical perspectives that have been brought to bear on literature written by black authors writing in Spanish. In an earlier work (see No. 16) I categorized trends into the subdivisions of Racist Authors and the Heritage of White Racial Consciousness; The Black as Social Symbol; and The Afro-Spanish American Author. I believe these perspectives mark tendencies in literary criticism of the Afro-Spanish American author that fall, for the most part, into what I now see as four main categories: black criticism, negristic or socio-negristic criticism, socialist or Marxist or nationalist criticism, and universal criticism, categories that have, in turn, racial overtones, sociological or ethnological connotations, and political implications (the latter with a decidedly nonracial emphasis).

Black criticism, which looks at black authors subjectively, that is, from a black ethnic point of view, reevaluates the black man's image in literature and in criticism and points if not toward the formulation of a black aesthetic in literature at least toward recognition of the role ethnicity plays in evaluating literature and criticism. Negristic or socio-negristic criticism interests itself mostly in the folkloric and atavistic aspects of black literature and in defending the Black. Marxist, socialist, and nationalist criticism emphasizes that revolutionary solidarity and *mestizaje* supersede the black element. This category, like the universal one, tends to whiten the black author by playing down his black ethnic identity. While much Afro-Spanish American criticism cannot be so rigidly classified, these positions are among those most easily recognized.

One could, in fact, prepare an ethnic, sociological, or ideological study of the critic by tracing critical positions on the black author in Spanish America. In literary criticism we take into account not only the author's experience or view and perhaps our own, reflected in the literature, but the critic's as well, often revealed through the position he takes in regard to the work confronted. A critic often sees not only what is there but also what he wants to see. Such flights of subjectivity are, however, understandable since a critic is rarely detached when reading a work analytically. The author was not detached when he wrote it and the reader will not be when he reads it. We should not, therefore, expect the critic, whether black or nonblack, to be totally detached when he analyzes it.

The annotated works in this bibliography, then, and the trends they represent, often point as much toward the critics as toward the works they discuss. For this reason I attempt in most cases to allow the critic's argument to speak for itself while keeping my opinions to a minimum. In this way the reader can draw his own preliminary conclusions about the works annotated without the imposition of my evaluative judgments.

Although this bibliography deals with works completed and underway, it also indicates what is forthcoming and, perhaps just as important, implies what remains to be done in the field of Afro-Hispanic studies. It becomes obvious, for example, that Cuba, Nicolás Guillén, and black poetry constitute the country, the author, and the genre that to date have received most of the critical attention.

One of the most notable trends in the last ten years has been the proliferation of studies of Blacks and black themes on university campuses. What is more, much of this university work is done by black students who, joined by a new generation of black scholars outside the university, are increasingly manifesting their interest in authentic black literature, that is, in literature written in Latin America by Blacks. Some of this dissertation work has not yet been published (see Nos. 76 and 89), but much of it is already appearing in whole or in part (see, for example, Nos. 102 and 304). Another obvious trend during this period, as I indicated in my "Recent Studies on Blacks in Hispanic Literature" (see No. 15), has been the move toward the book-length study which is, in part, anthology. This trend accounts for the publication of at least one and usually two, three, or four significant new books on Blacks in Hispanic literature annually since 1970. It should be noted, too, that new editions of works by black nineteenth- and twentieth-century authors are becoming increasingly more available (see, for example, Nos. 195, 251, 395, 490), which will facilitate the black author's incorporation into academic programs while giving him wider circulation and more visibility.

On the whole, general histories of literature and national histories of literature are not widely represented in this bibliography because, with the exception of largely repetitious references to Nicolás Guillén, black writers are not often mentioned in such works. Criticism in languages other than English and Spanish is, for the most part, excluded. I include a few items I have been unable to locate and annotate because I recognize their relevance to the subject and believe they should at least be mentioned. In Section III, I rarely repeat full bibliographical information for an entry that has been listed in full shortly before or in previous sections; such items are cross-referenced to the full listing. In the index I provide only the names of critics whose works I have annotated and not the names of the Afro-Spanish American authors themselves (unless they have also contributed critical work) since they are listed alphabetically in the table of contents, and geographically and chronologically in the lists following this introduction. A list of periodicals cited precedes the index.

Finally, although I focus on Afro-Spanish American authors in the strict sense of print literature, I annotate some of the work on José Vasconcelos ("El Negrito Poeta"), whose oral improvisations in eighteenth-century Mexico were written down by admirers. In like manner I annotate some of the recent studies on Lydia Cabrera. Her work on the Afro-Cuban folktale attests to the growing recognition of the importance of the role of the black oral tradition in Afro-Hispanic American literary history.

In fact, I should point out in closing that while Afro-Latin American writers are representative of such movements or styles as Romanticism, Naturalism, Modernism, even Vanguardism, oral literature, which they often incorporate into their formal literature, has always been important to them. Such black authors as Candelario Obeso in Colombia, Machado de Assis in Brazil, and Nicolás Guillén in Cuba insist that a national literature has to be built from the ground up, that is, from the popular sources the folk provide, for only there has a colonial mentality not taken root. In a forthcoming study I will explore the relationship of oral literature to a new humanism that is moving Latin American literature into a new stage of literary Americanism. In that study, which was inspired partly by many of the critics annotated in this bibliography, I will show that for the black writer in Latin America, humanism, literary Americanism, and literary Blackness are one and the same thing.

Authors by Country

COLOMBIA

Jorge Artel
Candelario Obeso
Arnoldo Palacios

Juan Zapata Olivella
Manuel Zapata Olivella

COSTA RICA

Quince Duncan

CUBA

Marcelino Arozarena
Nicolás Guillén
Juan Francisco Manzano
Nancy Morejón

Martín Morúa Delgado
Regino Pedroso
Gabriel de la Concepción Valdés
   ("Plácido")

ECUADOR

Nelson Estupiñán Bass
Adalberto Ortiz

Antonio Preciado

MEXICO

José Vasconcelos ("El Negrito
   Poeta")

PANAMA

Gaspar Octavio Hernández

Carlos Guillermo Wilson
   ("Cubena")

PERU

Nicomedes Santa Cruz

José Manuel Valdés

PUERTO RICO

Victorio Llanos Allende

xvii

URUGUAY

Pilar Barrios   Virginia Brindis de Salas

VENEZUELA

Juan Pablo Sojo

Authors by Period

EARLY LITERATURE (1821–1921)

Juan Francisco Manzano
Martín Morúa Delgado
Candelario Obeso
Gaspar Octavio Hernández

Gabriel de la Concepción Valdés
("Plácido")
José Manuel Valdés
José Vasconcelos ("El Negrito Poeta")

MAJOR PERIOD (1922–1949)

Marcelino Arozarena
Jorge Artel
Pilar Barrios
Virginia Brindis de Salas
Nicolás Guillén

Adalberto Ortiz
Arnoldo Palacios
Regino Pedroso
Juan Pablo Sojo

CONTEMPORARY AUTHORS (1950–)

Quince Duncan
Nelson Estupiñán Bass
Victorio Llanos Allende
Nancy Morejón
Antonio Preciado

Nicomedes Santa Cruz
Carlos Guillermo Wilson
("Cubena")
Juan Zapata Olivella
Manuel Zapata Olivella

The real *value of criticism lies in what it tells about the critic.*

Gerald Graff

I

GENERAL BIBLIOGRAPHIES

1. Acosta Saignes, Miguel. "Introducción al estudio de los repositorios documentales sobre los africanos y sus descendientes en América." *América indígena*, 29 (1969), 727-786.

    Attempts to provide for the first time a comprehensive guide to research material on the Black located in libraries and archives in Latin America. Names many useful bibliographies, journals, and other publications as well as unpublished documentation located in public and private libraries in most Latin American countries. Includes an extensive bibliography.

2. Arosemana Moreno, Julio. "Documentación relativa al negro en Panamá." *Lotería*, 44 (1969), 49-60.

    Lists the holdings on the Black in public, national, and university archives and libraries in Panama. Includes specialized and general works--books, articles, and chapters--where the Black in Panama is the subject.

3. Beltrán, Luis. "Los estudios afroamericanos y africanistas en Iberoamérica." *Cuadernos hispanoamericanos*, 97 (1974), 255-269.

    Laments that Afro-Ibero-American institutional research is not more widespread. Sets out to bring together what he sees as isolated activity in the field in Brazil, in Cuba, and in other Latin American countries. Calls for closer cooperation among specialists and further research which should include cooperation among African countries, Brazil, and the Spanish-speaking countries of Latin America.

4. Carvalho-Neto, Paulo de. "Bibliografía afro-ecuatoriana." *Humanitas. Boletín ecuatoriana de antropología*, 4 (1963), 5-19.

Does not set out to cover Afro-Ecuadorian poetry and works of fiction but includes, nevertheless, several Afro-Ecuadorian literary titles in the introduction.

5. Cobb, Martha K. *Afro-Hispania: A Research Bibliography of the Spanish-Speaking World.* Boston: G.K. Hall, forthcoming.

Provides a comprehensive annotated bibliography of literature by and about Blacks in Spain and Spanish America. Originally based on holdings in the Moorland Spingarn Collection on black literarure at Howard University.

6. Collantes, Ernesto Porras. *Bibliografía de la novela en Colombia, con notas de contenido y crítica de las obras y guías de comentarios sobre los autores.* Bogotá: Instituto de Caro y Cuervo, 1976. 888pp.

A bibliography that contains up-to-date entries on black novelists in Colombia. Emphasizes newspaper reviews and is a good source for local reception of the Afro-Colombian author.

7. Deschamps Chapeaux, Pedro. *El negro en el periodismo cubano en el siglo XIX: ensayo bibliográfico.* Havana: Ediciones R., 1963. 112pp.

Provides information on black authors in Cuba, some, such as Martín Morúa Delgado, prominent in literature as well as in journalism.

8. División de Filosofía y Letras, Departamento de Asuntos Culturales. Unión Panamericana. *Diccionario de la literatura latinoamericana. Ecuador.* Washington, D.C.: Unión Panamericana, 1962. 172pp.

Contains succinct commentaries on and some evaluation of various authors including leading Afro-Ecuadorian writers. Includes bibliography--largely references in literary histories--by and about the authors represented.

9. Fermoselle-López, Rafael. "The Blacks in Cuba: A Bibliography." *Caribbean Studies,* 12 (1972), 103-112.

Brings together many useful titles on the subject; includes a section on literature and literary criticism. Though hardly exhaustive, this is one of the most up-to-date general sources available on the black experience in Cuba.

10. Fernández Robaina, Tomás. *Bibliografía sobre estudios afro-americanos.* Havana: Biblioteca Nacional José Martí, 1968. 96pp.

    Lists items on the Black available in the National Library of Cuba. Organized alphabetically by author, includes as well a thematic listing of topics in many fields, including literature. Contains entries on Africa and America, especially on Cuba.

11. Fontvielle, Jean Roger. *Guide bibliographique du monde noir. Bibliographic Guide to the Negro World.* Yaounde, Cameroon: Federal University of Cameroon, 1970. 2 vols. 1173pp.

    A massive bibliography in two volumes that includes many entries relating to the black writer in Latin America, especially to the standard anthologies of black poetry. Contains a general listing by country and a second one alphabetically by author.

12. Granda, Germán de. "Materiales complementarios para el estudio socio-histórico de los elementos lingüísticos afroamericanos en el área hispánica (I. América)." *Thesaurus*, 26 (1971), 118–133.

    Oriented more toward America this bibliography supplements Granda's earlier general work (see No. 13). Has a narrative format with copious footnotes, some referring to black authors writing in Spanish, including Juan Pablo Sojo, Arnoldo Palacios, Manuel Zapata Olivella, Candelario Obeso, Jorge Artel, and Nicolás Guillén. Refers also to criticism on *negrista* poetry and to many standard works on *négritude* in Spanish American literature.

13. ————. "Materiales para el estudio sociohistórico de los elementos lingüísticos afroamericanos en el área hispánica." *Thesaurus*, 23 (1968), 547–573.

    Responds to need for compilation of general background material. Refers to previous bibliographies of this type, to studies on Africa, on slavery, and on black culture in individual countries. Useful to linguists and to the linguistic aspect of black poetry.

14. Heliodoro Valle, Rafael. "Para la bibliografía afroamericana." *Miscelánea en homenaje a Fernando Ortiz.* Havana: Ucar y García, Cía., 1955. Vol. I, pp. 1429–1466.

A substantial work that builds on James King's effort
(see No. 19) but lists many more entries, most of which
refer to literature and to literary criticism. Augments
greatly our knowledge of available material up to the
time of publication.

14a. Instituto de Investigaciones Sociales. *Bibliografía
afrocolombiana*. Popoyán: Universidad del Cauca, 1977.

15.   Jackson, Richard L. "Recent Studies on Blacks in Hispanic Literature." *The American Hispanist*, 2 (1977),
2-3.

Chronological review of comprehensive book-length
titles published in the 1970's, a period during which at
least one new title on Blacks in Hispanic literature appeared each year.

16.   ————. "Research on Black Themes in Spanish American
Literature." *Latin American Research Review*, 12 (1977),
87-103.

Outlines some of the recent trends in research on black
themes in Spanish American literature. Categorizes these
trends in the following subdivisions: racist authors and
the heritage of white racial consciousness; the Black as
social symbol; and the Afro-Hispanic author. Includes
extensive bibliography of creative and critical writings
related to black themes in Spanish American literature.

17.   Jahn, Janheinz. *Bibliography of Neo-African Literature
from Africa, America, and the Caribbean*. New York:
Frederick A. Praeger, 1965. 359pp.

A comprehensive bibliography of works Jahn classifies
as Neo-African literature, which he defines as literature
by black authors and by white authors whose "style" is
black. Covers creative works from Africa, America, and
the Caribbean with an extensive, though incomplete, section on Latin America. A useful compilation for research
on the Afro-Hispanic author, even though such black
writers as Marcelino Arozarena, Jorge Artel, Juan Pablo
Sojo, Nicomedes Santa Cruz, and Manuel Zapata Olivella,
among others, are missing.

18.   Kaiser, Ernest. "Recent Books." *Freedomways. A Quarterly Review of the Freedom Movement* (Spring 1961-).
Included in every issue.

For years Ernest Kaiser has been giving synoptic anno-
tations of books in "Recent Books," a regular section
which often includes comments on works by and about Afro-
Hispanic authors.

19. King, James Ferguson. "The Negro in Continental Spanish
     America: A Select Bibliography." *The Journal of Negro
     History*, 24 (1944), 547-559.

     Diverts attention away from the Caribbean and Brazil
     and toward what up to that time had been a relatively
     neglected area in Afro-Hispanic studies, namely, Con-
     tinental Spanish America. A short but thorough bibliog-
     raphy in its area of concentration. Useful background
     source to subsequent interest in research on the black
     theme in Continental Spanish American literature.

20. Latin American Studies Center. *Black Latin America. A
     Bibliography*. Los Angeles: California State University,
     1977. 73pp.

     Prepared under the direction of Timothy Harding in
     anticipation of the First Congress of Black Culture in
     the Americas held in Cali, Colombia, in August 1977.
     Designed to provide interdisciplinary information not
     only about the standard black areas but about the black
     population in such countries as Mexico, Uruguay, Costa
     Rica, and Argentina as well. Covers the humanities with
     much literature by and about black authors, although the
     emphasis is on the social sciences.

21. Pollak-Eltz, Angelina. "Bibliografía afrovenezolana."
     Montalbán, no. 5 (1976), 1023-1048.

     Charts increasing interest in Afro-Venezuelan research
     since the 1940's. Gives special recognition to the Afro-
     Venezuelan novelist Juan Pablo Sojo whom she also calls
     the "Father of Afro-Americanist research in Venezuela."

22. Porter, Dorothy. "African and Caribbean Creative
     Writings. A Bibliographic Survey." *African Forum*, 1
     (1966), 107-111.

     A brief survey that recognizes its limitations but one
     that includes reference to Janheinz Jahn's *Bibliography
     of Neo-African Literature* and to G.R. Coulthard's *Race
     and Colour in Caribbean Literature*.

23. Trelles, Carlos M. "Bibliografía de autores de la raza
     de color en Cuba." *Revista Cuba contemporánea*, 43
     (1927), 30-78.

     This first such bibliography of its kind was intended
     to illustrate progress Blacks had made in Cuba both
     during and following the abolition of slavery. Includes
     literary, journalistic, and political writings. Contains

402 entries including black journals and newspapers but
acknowledges that most of those mentioned are impossible
to locate.

24. Uriarte, Mercedes Lynn de. "Popular Culture in Latin
America: An Introductory Bibliography." *The Politics
of Culture. Proceedings of the Pacific Coast Council
on Latin American Studies*, 5 (1976), 141-191.

Contains a bibliographical section entitled "Afro-Latin
Culture," which lists such works as Lydia Cabrera's *El
monte*, José Luis Lanuza's *Morenada*, and Fernando Ortiz's
*Los bailes y el teatro de los negros en el folklore de
Cuba*.

25. Work, Monroe N. *A Bibliography of the Negro in Africa
and America*. New York: H.W. Wilson, 1928. Reprint.
New York: Octagon Books, Inc., 1965. 698pp.

This pioneering effort contains more than 17,000 entries
divided into two parts: "The Negro in Africa" and "The
Negro in America," with further subdivisions including
"The Negro and Literature in the West Indies and South
America" where works of Plácido and Juan Francisco
Manzano are listed.

II

GENERAL STUDIES AND ANTHOLOGIES

A. Full-length Studies and Anthologies

26. Ballagas, Emilio, ed. *Antología de la poesía negra hispanoamericana*. Madrid: Aguilar, 1935. 182pp. 2nd ed. 1944. 290pp.

An anthology of poems on black themes written largely by white Cubans but also includes selections by the Afro-Cubans Marcelino Arozarena, Nicolás Guillén, Regino Pedroso, and Ignacio Villa. Argues that white poets who write black poetry are able to capture the black spirit. Groups poems by theme to show diversity of black poetry.

27. ———, ed. *Mapa de la poesía negra americana*. Buenos Aires: Editorial Pleamar, 1946. 324pp.

Contends that a valid anthology of black poetry should include poetry by Blacks and by Whites on black themes. Includes selections from Walt Whitman, Henry Wadsworth Longfellow, and Sor Juana Inés de la Cruz, for example, as well as selections from many black authors writing in French, English, and Spanish.

27a. Barreda, Pedro. *The Black Protagonist in the Cuban Novel*. Translated by Page Bancroft. Amherst: University of Massachusetts Press, 1979. 179pp.

Prefaces his study with a summary review of the black theme in Cuban literature. Dismisses José Antonio Fernández de Castro's work *Tema negro en las letras de Cuba 1608-1935* (see No. 37) as inadequate because of its "lamentable omissions," among other deficiencies, but accepts this author's assertion that Gabriel de la Concepción Valdés ("Plácido") "denounced the purest Cubans of his day" to save his own life. Shows a pro-gressive enrichment in the characterization of the black

protagonist in contrast to a static stereotyping of the
black female character. Concludes that the novel about
Blacks in Cuba is *engagé* literature, but argues that the
black characters of José Antonio Ramos and Alejo
Carpentier, unlike earlier characterizations, take on
supraracial or universal significance.

28.   Calcagno, Francisco. *Poetas de color (Plácido, Manzano,*
      Rodríguez, Echemendía, Silveira, Medina). 4th ed.
      Havana: Imprenta Mercantil de los Herederos de Santi-
      ago, 1887. 110pp.

      First published partially in 1868 in a newspaper; was
      published again in 1878 and 1879, the latter an edition
      designed to buy the freedom of the slave poet José del
      Carmen Díaz. This first such study of black poets who
      wrote in Spanish largely details the life and works of
      Manzano and Plácido. Contains several appendices in-
      cluding work by Domingo Del Monte and poems by Plácido
      and Manzano.

29.   Cartey, Wilfred. *Black Images*. New York: Teachers
      College Press, Columbia University, 1970. xlv, 186pp.

      Provides an almost lyrical but thoroughly academic
      discussion of the black image largely in French and
      Spanish poetry of the Antilles. Moves from the early
      white poetry about Blacks in the Spanish Golden Age to
      twentieth-century black poetry. Dwells at length on
      Emilio Ballagas, Luis Palés Matos, and Nicolás Guillén.
      Contends that the poetry of the latter is not unrelated
      to the new black image created by the negritude poets
      writing in French. Recognizes the contribution of white
      writers in making known the black reality in America
      while pointing up the Black's new positive image, largely
      one of revolt, of his own design.

30.   Cobb, Martha K. *Harlem, Havana, and Haiti*. Washington,
      D.C.: Three Continents Press, 1979.

      Consolidates many of her ideas expressed in articles
      on concepts of literary blackness, bringing them to bear
      comparatively on the works of Langston Hughes, Jacques
      Roumain, and Nicolás Guillén.

31.   ————, ed. *Race and Literature in the Americas*. Wash-
      ington, D.C.: Porrúa, forthcoming.

      A collection that includes some essays that touch on
      the Afro-Hispanic author. See Nos. 103, 110, and 140
      below.

32. Coulthard, G.R., ed. *Caribbean Literature. An Anthology*.
    London: University of London Press, 1966. 127pp.

    Provides selections designed to suggest a Caribbean
    "sensibility" which relies on the permanence of African
    cultural features. Includes such established works as
    Nicolás Guillén's "Sensemayá," "Ballad of my two Grand-
    fathers," "Elegy," and "Ballad of the River Sprites."

33. ————. *Race and Colour in Caribbean Literature*. London:
    Oxford University Press, 1962. 152pp. First published
    in 1958 by the Escuela de Estudios Hispano-Americanos
    de Sevilla, under the title *Raza y color en la liter-
    atura antillana*. 178pp.

    Analyzes the theme of race and color in the literature
    of the Spanish, French, and British Caribbean. Recog-
    nizes Nicolás Guillén as one of the most original writers
    in Latin America who has successfully adapted the manner
    and rhythms of Afro-Cuban popular songs to "protest"
    literature. Deals both with white writers and with black
    authors who have written on the factors of race and color
    in the Caribbean countries. Ranges from the Cuban anti-
    slavery novel to recent literature concerned with social
    and psychological problems created by those factors.

34. Cyrus, Stanley, ed. *El cuento negrista sudamericano.
    Antología*. Quito: Editorial Casa de la Cultura Ecua-
    toriana, 1973. 215pp.

    This collection of *negrista* stories is the only one of
    its kind. Includes a substantial number of short stories
    by Afro-Hispanic authors. Especially useful in this
    collection are the up-to-date introductions that precede
    the stories. In brief introduction, rejects as pejora-
    tive the term *negroide* and settles on *negrista*, which
    admits literature on black themes by nonblack authors.

35. DeCosta, Miriam, ed. *Blacks in Hispanic Literature:
    Critical Essays*. Port Washington, N.Y.: Kennikat
    Press, 1977. 157pp.

    The first collection ever of critical essays "by a
    group of distinguished black scholars" on Afro-Hispanic
    literature, many of them, like DeCosta herself, set on
    structuring a new critical framework for the analysis
    of this literature, one that takes into account the re-
    lationship between literature and black history, culture,
    and ideology. Introduction calls for more use of black
    literary theorists in the United States as points of

departure for the black critic of Afro-Hispanic literature and culture and for more systematic comparison and
contrast of African and diasporic cultures.

36. Estupiñán Tello, Julio. *El negro en Esmeraldas.* Quito:
    Talleres Gráficos Nacionales, 1967. 175pp.

    Gives sociological interpretation of the black contri-
    bution to Ecuadorian culture. Contends that the over-
    riding characteristic of the Black in the province of
    Esmeraldas is his love of liberty, a trait that is re-
    flected in the literature of the area. Includes as il-
    lustration many literary selections from black writers
    of Esmeraldas, among them the well-known authors Adalberto
    Ortiz, Nelson Estupiñán Bass, and Antonio Preciado, and
    others not so well known.

37. Fernández de Castro, José A. *Tema negro en las letras
    de Cuba 1608-1935.* Havana: Editorial Mirador, 1943.
    95pp.

    Studies the black theme up to the year 1935. Begins
    his study by supporting the theory that the first Blacks
    in the New World came not from Africa but from Spain.
    Sees no literature by Blacks in Cuba before the publica-
    tion of Manzano's first books. Contends that early in-
    tellectuals despised Plácido because he did not attempt
    to rise above or protest his low position in society.
    Studies the work of other black writers and journalists
    in Cuba, particularly that of the young Nicolás Guillén.

38. Fernández de la Vega, Oscar, and Alberto Pamies, eds.
    Iniciación a la poesía afro-americana. Miami: Ediciones
    Universal, 1973. 213pp.

    Supports Ruiz del Vizo's theory (see No. 68) that there
    is a New School of Black Poetry composed by Cubans, both
    in Cuba and in exile. This is one of the few up-to-date
    volumes on this new poetry. It is as well a handy col-
    lection of hard-to-get studies of landmark value in the
    historiography of the Black in Hispanic literature. An
    intelligent and useful reference book, complete with im-
    portant dates, extensive (but by no means complete) lists
    of principal authors, and charts that map the development
    and thematic trajectory of black poetry in Hispanic
    America.

39. González, José Luis, and Mónica Mansour, eds. *Poesía
    negra de América.* Mexico: Ediciones Era, 1976. 474pp.

Tries to be thoroughly comprehensive by covering black
poetry written by Blacks and by Whites from early times
to the present in four different languages. A long comparative introduction by Mónica Mansour sets out differences in social and literary history that exist among
the four language regions represented--Spanish, English,
French, and Portuguese--insofar as the Black is concerned.
Contends that *mestizaje* has been a stronger component in
Spanish America than in Brazil. Says there is a differ-
ence in "sensibility" in the black poetry around the
Americas and that black poetry in Iberoamerica is a poetry *on* and *for* Blacks whereas in English and French
America black poetry is a poetry *by* Blacks. Argues that
mestizaje has diluted black poetry in Iberoamerica where,
she says, expressing this *mestizo* reality and joining in
the struggle against imperialism are more urgent.

40. González-Pérez, Armando, ed. *Antología clave de la
    poesía afroamericana.* Madrid: Ediciones Alcalá, 1976.
    288pp.

    Relegates black poetry in Portuguese, French, and
    English to a long appendix; the bulk of the anthology is
    given over to black poetry written in Spanish. Divides
    this part of the anthology into three sections with the
    third "Major Period" further subdivided into *Iniciadores*,
    Impulsores, and *Continuadores*. This last subsection in-
    cludes recent black poetry.

41. ————. *Poesía afrocubana última.* Milwaukee: Center
    for Latin America. University of Wisconsin, 1975.
    27pp.

    Gives Nicolás Guillén credit for the international
    success and recognition Afro-Cuban poetry has enjoyed.
    Evaluates new Afro-Cuban poetry written inside and out-
    side of Cuba since the Revolution. Sees a rebirth of
    interest since 1959 by both groups in the African cul-
    tural heritage and its influence on Cuban letters.

42. Guirao, Ramón, ed. *Orbita de la poesía afrocubana 1928-
    1937.* Havana: Ucar, García y Cía., 1938. 196pp.
    "Introducción" reprinted in *Iniciación a la poesía
    afro-americana.* Edited by Oscar Fernández de la Vega
    and Alberto Pamies (see No. 38), pp. 92-104.

    Unlike later anthologies of this type gives ample sam-
    ples of black folk poetry and black slave poetry (of
    Juan Francisco Manzano) together with black poetry

written by black and nonblack authors in the twentieth
century. Recognizes in the introduction but does not
include in the anthology antecedents from Spain's Golden
Age. Reviews black themes in Europe but sees Afro-Cuban
poetry as more tied to the national history and culture
of Cuba where the Black has been a decisive factor since
1521. Recalls the presence of several slave poets in
addition to Manzano.

43. Hernández Franco, Tomás. *Apuntes sobre poesía popular
    y poesía negra en las Antillas.* San Salvador: Publi-
    caciones del Ateneo de El Salvador, 1942. 72pp.

    Chooses, among others, the eighteenth-century unlettered
    black Dominican poet Meso Manica to illustrate Antillian
    popular poetry. Argues that, though forgotten today,
    the poetry of this shoemaker by trade has contributed
    much to American folklore. Argues further that black
    poetry in this century is really mulatto poetry and that
    Nicolás Guillén's poetry is written from within a mulatto
    soul but is a poetry that conveys, nevertheless, black
    grief through white poetic expressive techniques.

44. Inclán, Josefina. *Ayapá y otras Ota'n Iyebiye' de Lydia
    Cabrera (notas y comentarios).* Miami: Ediciones Uni-
    versal, 1976. 109pp.

    One of the several recent studies of the black oral
    folktale recreated by Lydia Cabrera. Agrees that there
    is a difference between *negrismo* and negritude and con-
    tends that Lydia Cabrera was a pioneer in what was later
    to be called negritude.

45. Jackson, Richard L. *The Black Image in Latin American
    Literature.* Albuquerque: University of New Mexico
    Press, 1976. 174pp.

    Explores prose and poetry by black and nonblack writers
    in the Caribbean and on the Spanish American mainland.
    Argues that Latin American literature reflects a strong
    tradition of racism and that *mestizaje* is another legacy
    of racism in that it means the destruction of black
    identity through cultural fusion and racial amalgamation.
    Explores the concept of negritude as it has developed in
    Latin America. Contends that in Latin America there is
    a rejection of the more mystical aspects of the concept
    and more emphasis on the racial, cultural, and histori-
    cal realities of the black experience in the New World.

46. ————. *Black Writers in Latin America.* Albuquerque: University of New Mexico Press, 1979. 254pp.

Picking up where *The Black Image in Latin American Literature* left off, traces through chronological over-view the development of black self-awareness or the Black as author from the controlled expression of the black writer of slavery times to the more assertive and aggressive black literature of our day. Though dealing more with the thematics than with the poetics of liter-ary blackness, certain stylistic, lyric, structural, and narrative devices are highlighted when they facilitate understanding of the black writer and of problematics of literary blackness in Latin America.

47. Jahn, Janheinz. *A History of Neo-African Literature. Writing in Two Continents.* Translated by Oliver Coburn and Ursula Lehrburger. New York: Farber and Farber Ltd., 1968. 301pp.

Traces the development of Neo-African literature from early times to the late 1960's. Gives some attention to Latin America and to poetic Negroism in Cuba. Dis-cusses the stylistic achievement of Nicolás Guillén and Marcelino Arozarena. Insists in this volume that liter-ature cannot be classified by the author's complexion or birthplace, that the color of an author's skin is not enough to decide the literary family he belongs to, and that literature can only be classified by style and by the attitudes revealed.

48. ————. *Muntu. An Outline of the New African Culture.* Translated by Marjorie Grene. New York: Grove Press, Inc., 1961. 269pp.

Attempts to present a systematic exposition of what he calls Neo-African culture built on European and tradi-tional African components. Tries to determine what is "really African" and what is not by measuring standards proper to African culture. Includes a chapter on *rumba* rhythm in lyric poetry with special attention to Marcelino Arozarena's poem "Caridad."

49. ————, ed. and trans. *Rumba Macumba. Afrocubanische Lyrik.* München: Carl Hauser Verlag, 1957. 77pp.

Calls his anthology Afro-Cuban poetry but includes black poetry from other countries such as Ecuador and Uruguay. One of the few anthologies to include poetry by the Afro-Uruguayan poet Virginia Brindis de Salas.

50. Johnson, Lemuel. *The Devil, the Gargoyle, and the
     Buffoon. The Negro as Metaphor in Western Literature.*
     Port Washington, N.Y.: Kennikat Press, 1969. 185pp.

     A comparative study that, for the most part, criticizes
     white writers who have written on the black theme in
     English, French, and Spanish. Focuses also on the black
     response of Langston Hughes, Nicolás Guillén, and Aimé
     Césaire to the white world. Analyzes the Black carica-
     tured as devil, gargoyle, and buffoon in English, French,
     and Spanish literature, underlining the negative, if not
     racist, nature of these literatures. Questions the cred-
     ibility of much of the literature on black themes in the
     Western world.

51. Latino, Simón, ed. *Antología de la poesía negra.* Buenos
     Aires: Cuadernillos de Poesía, 1963. 40pp.

     Argues that Blacks are in a better position to write
     an authentic black poetry that expresses the sentiments
     of the black race but acknowledges that Whites can write
     on black themes as well. Believes black poetry was on
     the wane after the advent of the Cuban Revolution and
     after the gains Blacks made in the 1960's in the United
     States. Asserts that such poetry now is more social
     than racial. Anthology is small but includes represen-
     tative poems by and about Blacks written in English,
     French, and Spanish, from Candelario Obeso to Nicolás
     Guillén.

52. Mansour, Mónica. *La poesía negrista.* Mexico: Ediciones
     Era, 1973. 279pp.

     Covers much the same ground as other similar works but
     is, nevertheless, unique in that it is more study than
     anthology. More detailed in some areas (Colonial and
     nineteenth century, for example) than most works, but
     less so in other areas. Is very specific in distin-
     guishing between *poesía negrista* and *poesía de la negri-
     tud,* though she errs in limiting negritude to African
     and American literature in French and English only. In-
     cludes several controversial statements, for example,
     regarding Plácido, Candelario Obeso, and José Martí.

53. Mondéjar, Publio L., ed. *Poesía de la negritud (anto-
     logía).* Madrid: Editorial Fundamentos, 1972. 143pp.

     Does not include any selections from Afro-Hispanic
     authors but refers several times in the introduction to

"the black Nicolás Guillén." Refers also to the historical role of poetic Negroism in Cuba as antecedent to
French negritude.

54. Morales, Jorge Luis, ed. *Poesía afroantillana y negrista:*
Puerto Rico, República Dominicana, Cuba. Río Piedras:
Editorial Universitaria, Universidad de Puerto Rico,
1976. 276pp.

Reviews black theme in general and focuses on black
poetry in the Spanish Antilles in particular. Argues
that Nicolás Guillén's poetry touches us more deeply
than that of others from Cuba, Puerto Rico, and the
Dominican Republic. Includes, perhaps for the first time
in an anthology anywhere, selections from the black mu-
sician Victorio Llanos Allende, who has been called Puerto
Rico's leading black poet.

55. Morales Oliver, D. Luis. *Africa en la literatura*
española. Madrid: Consejo Superior de Investigaciones
Científicas, 1957. 3 vols. 99pp., 114pp., 106pp.

Surveys in three volumes the theme of Africa from An-
tiquity to the present with some brief comments on the
African sound in the poetry of Nicolás Guillén.

56. Moreno Fraginals, Manuel, ed. *Africa en América Latina.*
Mexico: Siglo Veintiuno Editores, y UNESCO, Paris,
1977. 436pp.

A UNESCO-sponsored volume reminiscent of an earlier
one, *Introducción a la cultura africana en América Latina*
(Paris: UNESCO, 1970), but much larger and more ambitious.
Contains seventeen essays, some of them commissioned especially for this volume, including several that mention
or discuss the black writer in Latin America. M. Moreno
Fraginals contributes an introduction but argues, para-
doxically, that seeking traces of the Black in Latin
America is not as important as seeing how social groups
of all races have contributed to the creation of the
societies of which they are a part.

57. Noble, Enrique, ed. *Literatura afro-hispanoamericana:*
poesía y prosa de ficción. Lexington, Mass.: Xerox
Publishing, 1973. 200pp.

Designed partly as a reading text for intermediate
courses as well as for more advanced courses and seminars
in literature. Also distinguished by its organization,
which is structured around themes or topics rather than

by author or country. This presentation has value in
most cases, though the many typographical errors and
misspellings detract from the overall quality of the
work. Complete with extensive footnotes and vocabulary,
this anthology is a useful selection of prose and poetry,
even though one could argue with Noble's choices and ex-
clusions in both genres.

58. *Nouvelle somme de poésie du monde noir.* *Présence*
    Africaine (Paris), no. 57 (1966), 1-574.

    A special issue containing black poetry from Africa
    and America. From the Hispanic world only Cuba, classi-
    fied as Central America, is represented. Selections here
    include "Los heraldos negros," Nancy Morejón's hommage to
    César Vallejo.

59. Ortiz Oderigo, Nestor. *Aspectos de la cultura africana*
    en el Río de la Plata. Buenos Aires: Editorial Plus
    Ultra, 1974. 200pp.

    Provides not only extensive samples of the black pres-
    ence in the oral tradition of the River Plate area but
    illustrations from written literature as well. A good
    example of the latter is the poem "La voz del tamboril"
    of the Afro-Uruguayan poet Pilar Barrios, which high-
    lights the importance of the African drum in Afro-Uru-
    guayan culture. Gives numerous examples of the *pregón*,
    for which the Afro-Uruguayan poet Virginia Brindis
    de Salas is well known.

60. Pereda Valdés, Ildefonso, ed. *Antología de la poesía*
    negra americana. Santiago de Chile: Ediciones Ercilla,
    1936. 155pp. Reprint. Montevideo: B.U.D.A., 1953.
    218pp.

    Recognizes that authentic black poetry goes beyond di-
    alect and "slang" and roots itself in black psychology.
    Sees Alain Locke, Sterling Brown, and Langston Hughes as
    the leading black poets in the United States, where, he
    says, the best black poetry is written. Contends that,
    with the exception of Brazil and Cuba, black poetry in
    other countries pales by comparison. Singles out Nicolás
    Guillén and introduces the poetry of a "new figure," the
    Afro-Uruguayan poet Pilar Barrios.

61. ———. *El negro en el Uruguay, pasado y presente.*
    Montevideo: Revista del Instituto Histórico y Geográfico
    del Uruguay, 1965. 300pp.

Historical overview of the Black in Uruguay with chapters on his economic, social, and literary situation
today. Discusses discrimination in Uruguay and includes
a chapter on Afro-Uruguayan writers and intellectuals
with useful comments on the black press in that country.
Recognizes that there are few black writers in Uruguay
but gives information about several of them with brief
excerpts from the poetry of José Suárez and Juan Julio
Arrascaeta. Contends that the black writer in Uruguay
has been faced not only with discrimination and prejudice
but with indifference as well.

62.   ————, ed. *Lo negro y lo mulato en la poesía cubana.*
      Montevideo: Ediciones Ciudadela, 1970. 166pp.

Defends African influence in Cuban music, folklore, and
literature. Does not see any rebellious sentiment in
early black slave poetry or any "black" poetry at all
until Nicolás Guillén. Accepts that black poetry is,
in part, a white invention. Argues that there is a
black poetry and a poetry about Blacks. Recognizes that
authentic black poetry is on the increase despite what
he sees as class prejudices holding the Black back. Believes this authentic black poetry is mulatto and social
in Cuba, though thoroughly grounded in race. Extensive
commentary about and selections from black and white
authors in Cuba. One of the few books where black writers
are grouped and studied at length, albeit primarily limited to Cuba and to Arozarena, Pedroso, and Guillén.

63.   Perera, Hilda. *Idapo: el sincretismo en los cuentos
      negros de Lydia Cabrera.* Miami: Ediciones Universal,
      1971. 118pp.

Moves away from the study of black themes in written
literature and toward a consideration of black literature in the oral tradition, particularly in Cuba where
Lydia Cabrera's many collections of Afro-Cuban folktales
have placed her in the forefront of literary and folkloric investigators in this field.

63a. Primer Congreso de la Cultura Negra de las Américas.
      Conclusiones, recomendaciones y proposiciones. Cali,
      Colombia: Fundación Colombiana de Investigaciones
      Folklóricas, 1977. 53pp.

Proposes that the Institute of Afro-Colombian Research
take the lead in publishing works by black authors. The
recommendation considers such a move necessary because of

past discrimination in America against the publication
of black literature and because of the present need to
present a vigorous and positive image of the black man
both in literature and in the arts. Argues that black
literature should cultivate formal beauty but without
losing sight of the racial element. The Conference also
recognized the impact of the black oral tradition on New
World literature, paid homage to Luis Palés Matos in
appreciation of the attention he gave to the black theme
in his work, and commissioned a Hymn for New World
Blacks. Among other recommendations the Conference pro-
posed the creation of a Pan-Afro-American Society for
Black Culture.

64.   Rabassa, Clementine, and Gladys Seda-Rodríguez, eds.
      Studies in Afro-Hispanic Literature. Vol. I. New
      York: Medgar Evers College of the City University of
      New York, 1977. 100pp.

      The first of what could become ongoing publication of
      papers presented at the Afro-Hispanic Literature Symposia
      held annually in New York. This volume collects papers
      read at the Second Symposium, held June 18, 1977. The
      papers focus on black themes and black authors in several
      Latin American countries and Africa, including Gaspar
      Octavio Hernández, Plácido, and Nicolás Guillén.

65.   Rout, Leslie B., Jr. *The African Experience in Spanish
      America: 1502 to the Present*. Cambridge: Cambridge
      University Press, 1976. 404pp.

      A fine historical overview that deals with past,
      present, and future problems of the Afro-Latino. Often
      provides insightful comments on such Afro-Hispanic liter-
      ary figures as Adalberto Ortiz, Nicolás Guillén, Manuel
      Zapata Olivella, and Arnoldo Palacios.

66.   Ruiz del Vizo, Hortensia, ed. *Black Poetry of the
      Americas. A Bilingual Anthology*. Miami: Ediciones
      Universal, 1972. 176pp.

      Contains poems in Spanish, some translated from French,
      English, and Portuguese. Short introduction maintains
      that Cuba has by far the most authentic and popular of
      all black poetry, which, she says, is characterized by
      musicality, color, happiness, and movement.

67.   ————, ed. *Black Poetry of the Americas*. Vol. II.
      Miami: Ediciones Universal, 1977.

68.   ————, ed. *Poesía negra del caribe y otras áreas*.
      Miami: Ediciones Universal, 1972. 168pp.

      Representation restricted to Spanish-speaking areas in
      America. Contains, like her other volumes, an abundance
      of poems on black themes written recently by Cuban poets
      in exile. Her volumes make the point that these poets
      constitute a New School of Black Poetry, one that gives
      the lie to pronouncements that black poetry as a move-
      ment flourished and died largely between the two world
      wars. Her books give significant recognition also to
      black poetry in Colombia, though she rejects at the same
      time (not too convincingly) Colombia's claim that their
      black native son, Candelario Obeso (1849-1884), was a
      precursor of *poesía negra* as we know it in the twentieth
      century.

69.   Salgués de Cargill, Maruxa. *Presencia del negro en las
      letras hispanoamericanas*. La Corolina (Jaen): San
      Juan de la Cruz, 1975. 126pp.

70.   Sánchez, Reinaldo, et al., eds. *Homenaje a Lydia Cabrera*.
      Miami: Ediciones Universal, 1978. 349pp.

      Edits testimonials to Lydia Cabrera and papers read in
      her honor at a special conference on Afro-American liter-
      ature held in Miami in November 1976. The volume includes
      papers on black themes in general and on black poetry,
      people, and theater in particular, with a special section
      that groups presentations specifically on the work of
      Lydia Cabrera.

71.   Sanz y Díaz, José, ed. *Lira negra*. Madrid: Aguilar,
      1945. 2nd ed. 1962. 413pp.

      One of the earlier anthologies. Gives ample represen-
      tation to Spanish writers who have written poetry on
      black themes. Sees the origin of black poetry in Spanish
      partly in the Golden Age and partly in popular black
      music. Considers black poetry to be an important and
      abundant body of literature that needs to be consolidated
      in anthologies. Argues for the mestizo interpretation
      of black poetry in Spanish including Nicolás Guillén's
      and believes the most authentic black poetry is written
      in the southern part of the United States.

72.   Toruño, Juan Felipe. *Poesía negra*. *Ensayo y antología*.
      Mexico: Osidiana, 1953. 198pp.

Contains a substantial introductory essay to an anthology of black poetry with selections by black and nonblack authors, in which he analyzes poetry, focusing on form and content.

73. Valdés-Cruz, Rosa E. *La poesía negroide en América.* New York: Las Américas Publishing Co., 1970. 257pp.

Comprehensive in scope with authors represented in Spanish and in Spanish translation from all over the Americas and from Spain. Has been a handy tool in the many literature courses that have introduced the Black into the Hispanic curriculum. The few objections made to this volume from time to time on academic and technical grounds do not undermine its basic usefulness, if one can overlook such generalities as "the Cuban Black is always ready for fun and fiesta."

74. ————. *Lo ancestral africano en la narrativa de Lydia Cabrera.* Barcelona: Editorial Vosgos, 1974. 113pp.

The second book-length study to analyze the Afro-Cuban folktales of Lydia Cabrera. This study, like Perera's, recognizes the strong "white hand" of Lydia Cabrera in the transpositions of these black oral tales into written, artistic form.

75. Zenón Cruz, Isabelo. *Narciso descubre su trasero: el negro en la cultura puertorriqueña.* 2 vols. Humacao: Editorial Furidi, 1975. 343pp., 430pp.

Startled the Puerto Rican reading public with his extensive study/anthology of the black Puerto Rican (a phrase Zenón Cruz prefers to Puerto Rican Black) and his literary image. It is an understatement to say that his critical examination or exposé of racism in Puerto Rican literature and society will have as much impact in that country as Arriví's well-known trilogy *Máscara puertorriqueña.* Comprehensive enough to become the standard reference for years to come on black literature and the black theme in Puerto Rico.

B. Articles, Shorter Studies, and Dissertations

76. Amis, Barry D. "The Negro in the Colombian Novel." Ph.D. dissertation, Michigan State University, 1970. 216pp.

Contributes to the increasing number of studies about
the Black as theme and author particularly in prose fiction on the Spanish American mainland. Says "novels ex-
amined were chosen on the basis of their artistic merit
and because they deal with the Negro." Shows that novels
by such black writers as Arnoldo Palacios and Manuel
Zapata Olivella represent various stages in the development of the Colombian novel and in the treatment of the
Black as a literary figure. Argues that Palacios' portrayal of Irra in *Las estrellas son negras* may be the
most accomplished portrayal of the Black in Colombian
fiction, that Manuel Zapata Olivella is perhaps the only
Colombian author who has conceptualized the plight of the
Colombian Black on an international plane, and that
black authors have achieved the most understanding portrayal of black characters in Colombia.

77. Amor, Sister Rose Teresa. "Afro-Cuban Folktales as In-
     corporated into the Literary Tradition of Cuba." Ph.D.
     dissertation, Columbia University, 1969. 212pp.

     Studies the literary value of black folktales, myths,
and legends that black slaves brought to Cuba from
Africa. Though dealing with the oral tradition, recognizes that the Black has played an important role in
Cuban literary history both as author and theme. Presses
for more in-depth future studies on the black heritage
expressed in Afro-Cuban folktales.

78. Arango, Manuel Antonio. "La afirmación del negro en la
     literatura antillana." *Letras nacionales* (1963), 70-
     78.

     Largely a summary of G.R. Coulthard's *Race and Colour
in Caribbean Literature* (see No. 33).

79. Arróm, José Juan. "La poesía afrocubana." *Revista
     iberoamericana*, 4 (1942), 379-411.

     Says that the slave poet Manzano wrote verse that was
white in form but black in lament. Dismissed Plácido as
a poet who catered to white taste and money. Generalizes
that Blacks are childlike, happy-go-lucky, musical, su-
perstitious, and earthy people for whom women exist only
from the waist down.

80. Ballagas, Emilio. "Poesía afro-Cubana." *Revista de la
     Biblioteca Nacional de Cuba. Segunda serie*, 2 (1951),
     6-18. Reprinted in *Iniciación a la poesía afro-ameri-*

cana. Edited by Oscar Fernández de la Vega and
Alberto Pamies (see No. 38), pp. 78-87.

Considers Candelario Obeso to be one of the precursors
of Afro-Cuban poetry, though the Afro-Colombian was
never in Cuba. Accepts that *mestizaje* is the distinctive
characteristic of Afro-Cuban poetry and that one does
not have to be a Black to write good black poetry. Contends that the appearance of the poetry of Nicolás
Guillén in 1930 represented a great moment in Afro-Cuban
poetry because of its quality, which has not been sur-
passed. Sees Afro-Cuban poetry as part of a wider continental movement of Afro-American poetry.

81.   ————. "Situación de la poesía afroamericana." *Revista
      cubana*, 21 (1946), 5-60. Reprinted in *Iniciación a la
      poesía afroamericana*. Edited by Oscar Fernández de la
      Vega and Alberto Pamies (see No. 38), pp. 37-86.

Recognizes that black poetry in America is not a pure
African phenomenon but a transplanted one that comes under
the heading of creative *negrismo*, a general artistic
movement that includes black prose, sculpture, and paint-
ing. Sees need for more stylistic studies of negristic
poetry with more focus on poetics than on politics. Argues that pure African poetry has no need to be color
conscious or socially aware, unlike black poetry in the
Americas where slavery, discrimination, and *mestizaje*,
for example, become themes expressed through African stylistic means in European languages. Includes among his
conclusions that black poetry in America is mulatto, that
Blacks are not less intelligent than Whites, that Blacks
have been an influence wherever they have been brought,
and that black poetry becomes universal through Nicolás
Guillén.

82.   Bangou, Henry. "La influencia de Africa en las literaturas
      antillanas." *Casa de las Américas*, 10 (1969), 126-131.

Argues that there is more than one kind of negritude
and that the Cuban version derives from a humanistic impulse that years of Socialist government have made possible in the country.

83.   Baquero, Gastón. "Sobre la falsa poesía negra: tres
      notas polémicas." *Darío, Cernuda y otros temas poéticos*.
      Madrid: Editora Nacional, 1969, pp. 209-218.

Announces his intention in the title: to be polemical.
Judges black poetry in the Americas, until the appearance

of Aimé Césaire, to be one of the most painful and hypocritical forms of anti-black racism. Says Fernando Ortiz
was the black man's worst enemy because of what Baquero
calls Ortiz's pseudo-scientific views and his anachron-
istic vision of Blacks not as Cubans but as inferior and
savage Africans. Says Nicolás Guillén put this kind of
image behind him with his later social poetry.

84. Barreda, Pedro. "La caracterización del protagonista
    negro en la novela cubana." Ph.D. dissertation, State
    University of New York at Buffalo, 1969. 287pp.

    Takes a chronological approach and classifies the novels,
    which he analyzes aesthetically, by generations beginning
    with the stereotyped images of the Black in the abolition-
    ist novels, including Manzano's *Autobiografía*. Concludes
    with a discussion of the *negrista* narrative of Alejo
    Carpentier. Argues that Manzano and Morúa Delgado aspired
    only to be Cuban with no ethnic or racial classification.

85. Blomberg, Héctor Pedro. "La negra y la mulata en la
    poesía americana." *Atenea*, 80 (1945), 4-21.

    Reviews the treatment of black and mulatto women in
    Ildefonso Pereda Valdés's *Antología de la poesía negra
    americana*, which contains poems by such black authors as
    Countee Cullen, Langston Hughes, "Plácido," and Marcelino
    Arozarena. Also highlights the black presence during the
    time of Rosas, when the black woman played an important
    role in the history of Argentina, one reflected in the
    popular literature of the mid-nineteenth-century period.

86. Boj, S. "La poesía negra en Indoamérica." *Sustancia*,
    1 (1940), 591-608.

    Argues that black poets in Latin America are not as
    revolutionary in their thinking as black poets in North
    America. Affirms that the study of black poetry in what
    he calls Indoamerica must include the works of Nicolás
    Guillén and Marcelino Arozarena. One of the earliest
    studies to devote more than a passing comment to the
    poetry of Arozarena, but considers Nicolás Guillén to be
    the most interesting of the black poets he studies. Con-
    cludes that Nicolás Guillén is not a revolutionary.

87. Boulware, Kay. "Woman and Nature in *negrismo*." *Studies
    in Afro-Hispanic Literature*. Vol. I. Edited by
    Clementine Rabassa and Gladys Seda-Rodríguez (see No.
    64), pp. 16-25.

Contends that the black woman's beauty did not become
an object of poetic expression until the advent of
negrismo in the twentieth century and that the transition
from a white- to a black-oriented approach to feminine
poetic expression can be found in the poetry of Nicolás
Guillén. Illustrates that the black woman identified
with nature is a recurring motif in negristic poetry.

88. Boyd, Antonio Olliz. "The Concept of Black Awareness as
     a Thematic Approach in Latin American Literature."
     Blacks in Hispanic Literature: Critical Essays. Edited
     by Miriam DeCosta (see No. 35), pp. 65-73.

     Contends that despite ambiguous racial categories, a
     black perspective exists in Latin American literature,
     one that should not be limited to Nicolás Guillén. Sees
     racial awareness in the Modernist poetry of Gaspar Octavio
     Hernández. Argues strongly for the primacy of point of
     view in determining ethnic awareness.

89. ————. "The Concept of Black Aesthetics as seen in
     Selected Works of Three Latin American Writers: Machado
     de Assis, Nicolás Guillén and Adalberto Ortiz." Ph.D.
     dissertation, Stanford University, 1975. 243pp.

     Contends that literary theories can be based on ethnic
     affiliation. Approaches representative black and white
     authors to test the relationship of ethnicity to aesthet-
     ics. Analyzes race-oriented material to determine the
     subjectivity and the objectivity of authors.

90. ————. "Latin American Literature and the Subject of
     Racism." *College Language Association Journal*, 19
     (1976), 566-574.

     Documents the presence of racism in the contemporary
     literature of Hispanic America. Contends that a black
     novelist such as the Afro-Colombian Arnoldo Palacios
     "vividly rejects the notion that the personal conflict
     of his central figure Israel is to be seen in terms of
     class rather than race."

91. ————. "The Black Protagonist in Latin American Liter-
     ature: A Study in Ethnic Identity/Cultural Assimilation."
     SECOLAS Annals (Southeastern Conference on Latin American
     Studies), 9 (1978), 14-33.

     Acknowledges that there are recent examples of the
     black theme principally by black Latin American authors
     but limits his study to three novels on the black theme
     by nonblack authors that appeared between 1920 and 1940.

92. ———. "Socioliterature and the Black Experience in
     Latin America." *The Black Sociologist*, 7 (1978), 4-12.

   Considers the author and his ambience to be basic to
understanding the black experience, especially in the
creative literature of Latin America where most white
writers tend to substantiate their racial biases while
black authors largely combat racist images.

93. Brathwaite, Edward Kamau. "The African Presence in
     Caribbean Literature." *Daedalus*, 103 (1974), 73-109.
     Reprinted in Spanish as "Presencia africana en la
     literatura del Caribe." *Africa en América Latina*.
     Edited by Manuel Moreno Fraginals (see No. 56), pp.
     152-184.

   Argues that African culture not only crossed the Atlantic
but once here survived and converted Caribbean culture
into one understood only in terms of African traditions.
Contends that Caribbean literature shows much African
expression and considers Nicolás Guillén's poetry to be
one example of African thematic and rhythmic influence.

94. Bronx, Humberto. "La novela colombiana en los últimos
     veinte años." *20 anos de novela colombiana*. Medellín:
     Editorial Granámerica, n.d., pp. 17-33.

   Identifies Arnoldo Palacios' *Las estrellas son negras*
as unique in its use of a "sordid naturalism" and includes Manuel Zapata Olivella among Colombian novelists
who are most accomplished stylistically.

95. Bueno, Salvador. "La canción del bongó: sobre la cultura
     mulata de Cuba." *Cuadernos americanos*, 106 (1976),
     89-106.

   Using as a point of departure Guillén's poem "La canción
del bongó," considers *mestizaje* both cultural and ethnic
to be Latin America's distinguishing feature within the
Third World, especially in Cuba. Calls Plácido a "white"
poet in his poetry since the black experience rarely
entered it.

96. ———. "Presencia negra en la literatura narrativa
     cubana." *Acta literaria* (Budapest), 13 (1971), 49-54.

   Asserts that Las Casas wrote the first protest literature in the New World, where the black theme in literature appeared very early. Includes Manzano's *Autobiografía* among the earlier distinctive works in this field,

and says that Martín Morúa Delgado's black novels contain
good examples of the incest theme in Cuban literature.

97. Cabrera, Rosa M. "La búsqueda de la identidad en la
     poesía afroantillana." *Homenaje a Lydia Cabrera.*
     Edited by Reinaldo Sanchez et al. (see No. 70), pp.
     111-121.

     Argues that Nicolás Guillén's poem "El apellido" is one
     of the best expressions of the black man's anguished
     search for his own name, origin, and identity, erased
     symbolically by the white man's surname which has been
     imposed on him. But sees Guillén's "Los dos abuelos" as
     acceptance and affirmation of a racial duality. Recog-
     nizes Regino Pedroso's identification with Blacks to be
     best expressed in his "Hermano negro."

98. Canfield, Martha L. "Precursores de la poesía negra."
     Razón y fábula, no. 21 (1970), 13-27.

     Considers her work to be the beginning of systematic
     study of black poetry in Latin America. Argues that
     black poetry even has its own tradition, though it is,
     at the same time, part of the larger literary history of
     the area. Identifies precursors and sees them within
     the generational scheme outlined by José Juan Arróm.
     Does not base selections on aesthetic merit alone, as
     she considers historical importance equally significant.
     Agrees with Arróm that black poetry is an offshoot of
     Vanguardism rather than a branch of Modernism. Sees
     black poetry dating back to the generation of 1834, which
     includes Plácido, and discusses the pioneering work in
     succeeding generations of Candelario Obeso and Pilar
     Barrios.

99. Castagnino, Raúl H. "Poesía negra de Hispanoamérica."
     *Escritores hispanoamericanos desde otros ángulos de
     simpatía.* Buenos Aires: Editorial Nova, 1971, pp. 291-
     314.

     Argues that the real impetus to blackness as an aes-
     thetic theme in this century came from Modernism in
     general and Rubén Darío in particular who wrote about
     Blacks in prose and in poetry. Defines Guillén's poetry
     as aristocratic but popular, aesthetically accomplished,
     though ideologically tinged.

100. Cobb, Martha K. "Africa in Latin America: Customs,
      Culture and Literature." *Black World*, 21 (1972), 4-19.

Discusses the black theme in Latin American literature
but largely highlights Afro-Hispanic authors--Plácido,
Manzano, José del Carmen Díaz, Morúa Delgado--and the
twentieth-century triumvirate: Marcelino Arozarena,
Regino Pedroso, and Nicolás Guillén. Emphasizes particularly the latter, whose poems are used to illustrate stylistic elements and black themes and to show the progres-
sion of black poets toward social protest.

101.   ————. "A Role for Spanish in the Humanities Program."
Hispania, 54 (1971), 302-307.

Contends that the fusion of many cultures on the Iberian
Peninsula and later in Spanish America, once understood,
can help bridge the problem of racial separation. Insists
that our class materials must move away from medieval
classics and incorporate nineteenth- and twentieth-century
works by Spanish Americans of African descent if we are
to succeed in creating a realistic new image of nonwhite
people. Suggests that such Afro-Americans as Plácido
should be better known to Americans.

102.   ————. "Concepts of Blackness in the Poetry of Nicolás
Guillén, Jacques Roumain and Langston Hughes." *College
Language Association Journal*, 18 (1974), 262-272.

Argues that similarities in the themes, images, and
techniques in the poetry of Nicolás Guillén, Jacques
Roumain, and Langston Hughes imply a Neo-African literature that crosses national and linguistic boundaries.
Conceptualizes the experiences of Blacks--confrontation,
dualism, identity, and liberation--into devices for or-
ganizing thematic patterns and imagery into the dynamics
of a black aesthetic in their works.

103.   ————. "Redefining the Definitions in Afro-Hispanic
Literature." *Race and Literature in the Americas*.
Washington, D.C.: Porrúa, forthcoming.

Takes a broad view toward black literature in the
Americas and recognizes Afro-Hispanic literature to be
a part of this totality with patterns and responses
similar to the black situation in the English- and
French-speaking areas of America. Underlying principles
useful in the interpretation of black literature fall
under the heading of conception (or the author's vision),
structure (or the way the author organizes his material
and uses language), theme, and style, all of which re-
veal and identify the black experience in America. Fo-

cuses for illustration on the works of Nicolás Guillén,
Adalberto Ortiz, and Manuel Zapata Olivella.

104. Coleman, Ben. "Black Themes in the Literature of the
      Caribbean." *The Rican: A Journal of Contemporary
      Puerto Rican Thought*, no. 3 (1973), 48-54.

      Affirms that the literature of a particular country or
      region reflects its society. Argues that this is es-
      pecially true in Cuba, Puerto Rico, Venezuela, Colombia,
      and other republics in the Caribbean where black themes
      and black characters and black linguistic habits are
      evident in the novel, the short story, and poetry.

105. Commetta Manzoni, Aida. "Trayectoria del negro en la
      poesía de América." *Nosotros*, 4 (1939), 196-212.

      Says Blacks were stronger than Indians and could do
      the hardest tasks without detriment to their health.
      Contends further that Blacks were docile and resigned
      and so happy they forgot all about being slaves or re-
      belling against their slave status. After making such
      statements she goes on to admit that although the Black
      was "just a slave," he did influence the New World with
      his songs, his music, and his blood. It is this black
      blood, she argues, that makes the poetry of Nicolás
      Guillén and Langston Hughes universal.

106. Coulthard, G.R. "Antecedentes de la negritud en la
      literatura hispanoamericana." *Mundo nuevo*, no. 11
      (1967), 73-77. Also published as "La negritud en la
      literatura hispanoamericana." *Revista de la Universi-
      dad de Yucatán*, 9 (1967), 60-70.

      Analyzes traces of negritude in the works of Nicolás
      Guillén, Luis Palés Matos, and Adalberto Ortiz that
      antedate the later explosion in the French Caribbean.
      While Palés Matos and Guillén are better known, Coult-
      hard believes that Ortiz is more profoundly black in
      his orientation than the other two.

107. ————. "The Emergence of Afro-Cuban Poetry." *Caribbean
      Quarterly*, 2 (1950), 14-17.

      Considers Nicolás Guillén to be the originator of the
      Afro-Cuban movement, Cuba's answer--in the absence of
      the Indian--to literary Americanism. Argues further
      that Nicolás Guillén, a serious protest poet, did not
      get bogged down in sensuality and the cult of the primi-
      tive.

108. DeCosta, Miriam. "Canebake and Cotton Field: Thematic Parallels between Afro-Hispanic and Afro-American Poetry." *South Atlantic Bulletin*, 41 (1975-76), 74-85.

Writes of similarities and intellectual symbiosis among negritude, *negrismo*, and the Harlem Renaissance and among Nicolás Guillén, Jacques Roumain, and Langston Hughes that transcend cultural differences. Believes the characteristics of Afro-Hispanic poetry can be analyzed or studied from three major perspectives: stylistic, cultural, and thematic, and contends that it is this latter category where Neo-African literatures have much in common, as Blacks in the diaspora viewed the larger society in much the same way despite differences in language, technique, styles, forms, and locale.

109. ————. "Social Lyricism and the Caribbean Poet/Rebel." *College Language Association Journal*, 14 (1972), 441-451. Reprinted in *Blacks in Hispanic Literature: Critical Essays*. Edited by Miriam DeCosta (see No. 35), pp. 114-122.

Sees themes of protest running throughout black oral poetry but not in black erudite expression until the advent of the Afro-Cuban poets: Nicolás Guillén, Marcelino Arozarena, and Regino Pedroso, whose approaches are different but whose message is the same, namely, a call to arms.

110. ————. "The Dialectic of Sex and Race in the Black South American Novel." *Race and Literature in the Americas*. Edited by Martha K. Cobb (see No. 31).

Appraises a subject that forms the core of many novels on black themes in Spanish America, particularly where the black woman, as in Adalberto Ortiz's *Juyungo*, is seen in stereotyped roles.

111. Del Monte, Domingo. "Dos poetas negros: Plácido y Manzano." *Humanismo y humanitarismo: ensayos críticos y literarios*. Havana: Editorial Lex, 1960. Also in Francisco Calcagno, *Poetas de color* (see No. 28), pp. 98-100.

Argues in this 1845 essay that since Plácido was free and almost white he had fewer obstacles to face than Manzano who was black and a slave for more than thirty years.

112. Depestre, René. "Las metamórfosis de la negritud en
      América." *Etnología y folklore*, no. 7 (1969), 43-54.

      Marxist interpretation of the search for black identity
      in America from slavery and its depersonalization to
      today, a search that after a long history of rebellion
      culminates in a modern progressive spirit of negritude.
      Understands negritude not in mystical terms but in the
      practical example of Nicolás Guillén and the Cuban
      Revolution which represents, he argues, a new point of
      departure for the Black in the New World.

113. ————. "Problemas de la identidad del hombre negro
      en las literaturas antillanas." *Casa de las Américas*,
      6 (1968), 19-28. Published in English as "Problems
      of Identity for the Black Man in Caribbean Literature."
      Translated by George Irish. *Caribbean Quarterly*, 19
      (1973), 51-61.

      Singles out the problem of identity or "coming to
      terms with oneself" as a major preoccupation of twenti-
      eth-century black writers. Believes that the problem
      in the Caribbean nations has been solved only in Cuba.
      Makes an important distinction between *negrismo* and
      negritude, one a movement primarily of white intellec-
      tuals, the other a movement more committed to the de-
      struction of myths and stereotypes of the Black. Con-
      trasts progressive negritude in Cuba, which is in har-
      mony with the Revolution, with Duvalier's negative
      negritude and with Senghor's mystical negritude.

114. ————. "Saludo y despedida a la negritud." *Africa en
      América Latina*. Edited by Manuel Moreno Fraginals
      (see No. 56), pp. 337-362.

      Places Nicolás Guillén squarely among those Latin
      American writers whose works reveal a search for the
      "formula of Americanism." Agrees with Fernández
      Retamar that racial sentiment in Guillén's poetry is
      linked to the historical essence of Cuba, the Caribbean,
      and America, and that Guillén's poem "Llegada" symbolizes
      this essence.

115. Domínguez, Ivo. "En torno a la poesía afrohispano-
      americana." *Cuadernos hispanoamericanos*, 107 (1977),
      125-131.

      Calls his article "Afro-Hispanic" to highlight this
      poetic activity outside the Caribbean in such countries
      as Argentina, Ecuador, Chile, Peru, and Uruguay. Sees

black poetry in three dimensions: folkloric, social
protest, and black beliefs or psychology, the least
treated in Afro-Hispanic research. Considers the black
theme to be the core of the work of Nicolás Guillén and
the fomenting of black pride his objective.

116. Drake, St. Clair. "The Black Diaspora in Pan-African
      Perspective." *The Black Scholar*, 7 (1975), 2-14.

      Raises some relevant research problems for scholars
      interested in the Afro-Hispanic author and in discover-
      ing the level of black consciousness in countries in
      Latin America where black communities persist. Sees
      the study of "false consciousness" and how it can be
      dissipated to be of crucial importance.

117. Duvalier, Vauquelin. "La poesía negroide de Cuba."
      Atenea, no. 145 (1937), 28-36.

      Argues that it would be a mistake to consider Plácido
      as Cuba's first racial poet since he did not write on
      Afro-Cuban themes. Contends that there is no repre-
      sentative black poet in Brazil and that Langston Hughes
      is the most complete black poet in the United States.
      Asserts that since Nicolás Guillén is the leading black
      poet in the Caribbean area, it is only natural to find
      in his work all of the basic themes and techniques that
      characterize black poetry.

118. Dzidienyo, Anani. "Activity and Inactivity in the
      Politics of Afro-Latin America." *SECOLAS Annals* (South-
      eastern Conference on Latin American Studies), 9 (1978),
      48-61.

      Though concerned with group manifestation of political
      activity by Afro-Latin Americans, gives significant
      attention to such individual Afro-Hispanic writers as
      Juan Zapata Olivella and his brother Manuel. Also fo-
      cuses on Edelma Zapata Olivella, a young black poet
      whose work also develops black themes, and on Nicomedes
      Santa Cruz.

119. Edwards, Flora M. "The Theater of the Black Diaspora.
      A Comparative Study of Black Drama in Brazil, Cuba,
      and the United States." Ph.D. dissertation, New York
      University, 1975. 298pp.

      Argues that black theater in the United States makes
      a political statement and is concerned with black iden-
      tity whereas in Latin America, Cuba, and Brazil in par-
      ticular, black theater is more closely related to the

overall struggle to establish a national identity.
Whatever the approach, though, contends that black
theater, "an intrinsic part of the struggle for human
dignity and freedom," in all three countries is a theater
of total commitment and direct communication. Concludes
that black theater in the Americas is neither African
theater in exile nor white theater in blackface.

120. Esquenazi-Mayo, Roberto. "Impacto de Africa en la liter-
      atura hispanoamericana." *Expression, Communication
      and Experience in Literature and Language*. Edited by
      Ronald G. Popperwell. London: Modern Humanities Re-
      search Association, 1973, pp. 135-137.

      Contends that the study of the Black in literature
      outside of the Caribbean has been neglected perhaps be-
      cause of prejudice. Demonstrates that the African in-
      fluence had spread around Latin America to such places
      as the River Plate area, Ecuador, Colombia, and Peru.

121. Estupiñán Bass, Nelson. "Apuntes sobre el negro de
      Esmeraldas en la literatura ecuatoriana." *Norte*, 7
      (1967), 101-109.

      Says aggressive pride has moved the Black into promi-
      nence where he has captured the attention of black and
      white novelists, poets, and painters in Esmeraldas--Ecua-
      dor's black province--especially since the 1930's. Il-
      lustrates his point by including some of his own verse
      and some black poetry by Adalberto Ortiz and Antonio
      Preciado.

122. Feijoo, Samuel. "Influencia africana en Latinoamerica:
      literatura oral y escrita." *Africa en América Latina*.
      Edited by Manuel Moreno Fraginals (see No. 56), pp.
      185-214.

      Contends that black oral literature has not been given
      the attention it deserves in such countries as Mexico,
      Peru, Ecuador, Colombia, and Venezuela. Argues also
      that the nineteenth-century black writer had become
      Americanized, more influenced by "white" Spanish liter-
      ature than by Africa. Recognizes the seditious nature
      of Plácido's poetry, the power of Manzano's *Autobio-
      grafía*, and the supremacy of Nicolás Guillén in the
      "black poetry" movement.

123. Fernández de Castro, José A. "El aporte negro de las
      letras de Cuba en el siglo XIX." *Revista crisol*

(Mexico) (1935), 271-290. Reprinted in *Revista bimestre cubana*, 38 (1936), 46-66.

Sees the thrust of his work as twofold: to study (1) the Black as author and (2) the Black as theme. Traces the theme from the first poem written on the Black in Cuba, and the Black as author from the colored poets Manzano and Plácido. Argues that Plácido was not involved in the Conspiración de la Escalera and believes he was despised by the intellectuals of his time for this reluctance to get involved. To Fernández de Castro, Plácido is unjustifiably famous. Completes his list of "black and mestizo poets of slavery times" by naming A. Baldomera Rodríguez, J.B. Estrada, Vicente Silveira, and José del Carmen Díaz, whom he rates as third- and fourth-class poets, to judge from the little of their work that is available. They are, he argues, worthy of admiration, however, considering the extraordinary difficulties they had to face. Mentions Morúa Delgado and the journalistic work of Rafael Serra and Juan Gualberto Gómez.

124. ————. "La literatura negra actual en Cuba (1902-1934). Datos para un estudio." *Estudios afrocubanos*, 4 (1940), 3-22.

Notes the absence of black writers with the exception of some black journalists in the early profusion of "black" literature at the beginning of this century in Cuba. But this changes, he affirms, with the advent of Nicolás Guillén. Considers *Sóngoro cosongo* (1931) to be Guillén's first book of "formal" verse. Mentions very briefly Regino Pedroso and Martín Morúa Delgado.

125. Fernández de la Vega, Oscar. "Origen del negrismo lírico antillano desde tres perspectivas." *Homenaje a Lydia Cabrera*. Edited by Reinaldo Sánchez et al. (see No. 70), pp. 131-138.

Approaches "Afro-Iberian" poetry through content, attitudes, and style. Rejects the terms *negra*, *mulata*, and *negroide* in favor of *negrista*. Does not limit black poetry to the period between the two world wars or to Cuba, and rejects Palés Matos and Alfonso Camín as sole initiators of *negrista* poetry, which, he says, even antedates the negritude of Césaire and Senghor. Asserts that black poetry is abundant in Puerto Rico and that the Hispanic emphasis of Plácido and the African emphasis of Candelario Obeso come together in the poetry of José Manuel Poveda who, thematically, is the true ini-

tiator, he argues, of *negrista* poetry as we know it in
this century.

126. Franco, Jean. "The Negro." *The Modern Culture of Latin
      America: Society and the Artist*. London: Pall Mall
      Press, 1967, pp. 131-140.

Discusses the new dignity accorded to the Black in
this century and names Nicolás Guillén the outstanding
poet of the Afro-Cuban movement. The poetry of this
movement, she contends, "takes us right away from the
Afro-Cuban cliché figure of the sensual rumba dancer."
Shows, through the example of Adalberto Ortiz, how a
literary fashion can give genuine artistic expression
to a hitherto silent section of a community.

127. Garcés, Ramón Lozano. "Dimensión universal del negro."
      Universidad de Antioquia (Medellín), 45 (1968), 5-27.

Reviews comprehensively black achievement in Africa and
America, particularly in Colombia. Contends that Blacks
have special talent in the arts and attempts to list
the most outstanding credits to the black race, including several Afro-Colombian writers.

128. García, Calixto. "El negro en la narrativa cubana."
      Ph.D. dissertation, City College of New York, 1973.
      387pp.

Devotes major chapters to white authors who wrote on
black themes in prose. Supplements his volume with
discussions of black oral tales collected by Lydia
Cabrera and Rómulo Lachatañeré and with a list of black
Spanish words "spoken" in the works discussed. Manzano
and Morúa Delgado are conspicuous by their absence from
a work of this kind. Mentions the latter only in passing.

129. Gilliam, Angela. "Black and White in Latin America."
      Présence Africaine, no. 92 (1974), 161-173.

Writes that black literature in the United States is
more plentiful than in Latin America. Recognizes, however, that such black writers in Latin America as Nicolás
Guillén and Nicomedes Santa Cruz are becoming more visible. Argues that to really know the black definition
of self in Latin America, though, one must delve into
the field of oral literature.

130. Gonzalez Contreras, Gilberto. "La poesía negra."
      Revista bimestre cubana, 37 (1936), 40-45. Reprinted

in *Iniciación a la poesía afro-americana*. Edited by
Oscar Fernández de la Vega and Alberto Pamies (see
No. 38), pp. 107-116.

Affirms that black poetry is cultivated mostly by
Whites but acknowledges Nicolás Guillén to be the best
poet of the genre, a reputation earned not through musical and rhythmic verse but through his revolutionary
and political emphasis in *West Indies Ltd*.

131. Gordils, Janice Doris. "La herencia africana en la
     literatura cubana de hoy." Ph.D. dissertation, New
     York University, 1976. 393pp.

Concludes that it is wrong to speak of a black literature or of an Afro-Cuban literature. Argues that it is
more exact to speak of this literature as one that at
every turn has coincided or answered to the wishes of
the larger society. Considers African religion to be
an important source for literature.

132. Graf, Henning. "Africa en América--Algunos aspectos de
     la simbiosis literaria afroamericana." *Humanitas*, 15
     (1974), 353-396.

Observes that the most obvious black contribution in
the New World is the biological one, which can be seen
in the mixed composition of the Latin American people
in certain countries. Reviews such white racist stereo-
types of Blacks as sensuality, happy-go-lucky nature,
love of bright colors, talkativeness, and imitative
behavior. Sees the ultimate development of Guillén's
poetry to be away from strict negritude and toward a
wider social and political poetry humanistically in-
clined. Does not distinguish between poetry by Blacks
and poetry about Blacks and sees such characteristics
of Afro-American poetry as integration, synthesis, and
cultural *mestizaje* as inherent in the term "Afro-American" itself.

133. Harth, Dorothy Feldman. "La poesía afrocubana, sus
     raíces e influencias." *Miscelánea de estudios dedi-
     cados a Fernando Ortiz*. Havana: Ucar y García. Vol.
     II, 1955, pp. 790-815.

Identifies freedom as the basic desire expressed in
Afro-Cuban poetry. Conjectures that Plácido's poetry
was a means of escape from his harsh existence, in the
same manner as Rubén Darío's. Considers the *jitanjáfora*
and linguistic innovation to be two of the outstanding

characteristics of black poetry especially in the work
of Nicolás Guillén whose most interesting poetry, she
says, is characterized by imitative dialect.

134. Henríquez Ureña, Max. "Poesía afrocubana." *Panorama
histórico de la literatura cubana.* Havana: Editora
Revolucionaria, 1967, pp. 374-378.

Agrees with Ramón Guirao that black poetry as a movement burnt itself out in Cuba between the years 1928
and 1937.

135. Herrera, Roberto. "La poesía afrocubana." *Charlas
literarias.* Miami: Ediciones Universal, 1972, pp.
19-32.

Despite his title, accepts Fernando Ortiz's term
poesia mulata as he, like Ortiz, sees black poetry as
the product of a fusion of the two races and two cultures: white Europe and black Africa. Also accepts the
generally held notion that Palés Matos interprets the
Black from the perspective of an outsider, of a "civi-
lized White," while Nicolás Guillén interprets him more
realistically and from within. Thinks that Marcelino
Arozarena is more erotic in his *rumba* poetry than Nicolás
Guillén and that Guillén's first black books, *Motivos
de son* (1930) and *Sóngoro cosongo* (1931), unlike scat-
tered poems and items of others, were the first solid
publications (books) on the black theme.

136. Jackson, Richard L. "Black Phobia and the White Aesthetic in Spanish American Literature." *Hispania*,
58 (1975), 467-480.

Surveys the literary manifestation of the heritage of
white racial consciousness in Spanish American literature. Gives as well examples of the rejection of this
white aesthetic in literature by writers of African
descent.

137. ————. "Black Song without Color: The Black Experience
and the Negritude of Synthesis in Afro-Spanish American Literature." *Inter-American Review of Bibliography*,
76 (1977), 143-161.

Argues that the black writer in Latin America was not
so seduced by song, dance, and musical rhythms that he
was unable to concern himself with civil rights, justice,
and freedom and with establishing bonds of racial solidarity with his black brothers around the world.

138.   ————. "Ethnicity and the Modernist Aesthetic in
       Panama." *Studies in Afro-Hispanic Literature*. Vol.
       I. Edited by Clementine Rabassa and Gladys Seda-Rod-
       ríguez (see No. 64), pp. 3-15.

       Argues that black awareness informs the aesthetics
       of black writers in Latin America even when those aes-
       thetics, as in the case of the Afro-Panamanian Gaspar
       Octavio Hernández, are diverted into an exaggerated
       cult of whiteness.

139.   ————. "The Ethnicity Factor and Afro-Latin American
       Literature." *Norte/Sur: Canadian Journal of Latin
       American Studies*, 3 (1978), 104-118.

       Sees an ethnicity factor at work in Afro-Latin American
       literature where literary blackness operates as the
       overriding organizing principle. Affirms that there is
       a very real black experience in Latin America which is
       reflected in what can be called a literature of a black
       experience as opposed to a literature of a black aes-
       thetic.

140.   ————. "Prospects for a Black Aesthetic in Latin
       America." *Race and Literature in the Americas*. Edited
       by Martha K. Cobb (see No. 31).

       Contends that there is little "radical" black litera-
       ture in Latin America that specifically supports black
       nationalism and a concomitant militancy. Argues, how-
       ever, that there is much literature written there by
       Blacks which is authentically and identifiably black,
       certainly enough that can be distinguished from black
       literature written by nonblack authors.

141.   ————. "Racial Identity and the Terminology of Liter-
       ary Blackness in Spanish America." *Revista chicano-
       riqueña*, 5 (1978), 43-48.

       Believes that interest in the study of Afro-Hispanic
       literature is higher now than it was in the celebrated
       high period of *poesía negra* in the 1930's and 1940's.
       This is so partly because more black scholars than ever
       before are focusing attention on the black experience
       in Spanish America, particularly with a high degree of
       interest in authentic black literature, that is, in
       literature by Blacks in Spanish America rather than in
       Spanish American literature simply on black themes.
       Argues that this increased interest has intensified a
       need and a desire for more precise interpretations to

the problem of terminology and to the problem of racial
identity.

142. Jahn, Janheinz. "Poetry in Rumba Rhythms." Ulli Beier,
      *Introduction to African Literature. An Anthology of
      Critical Writings on African and Afro-American Litera-
      ture and Oral Tradition.* London: Longmans, 1967, pp.
      139-150.

      Argues that the sharp accentuation of Spanish and the
      purity of its short sonorous vowels allow for the easy
      incorporation of African rhythms and vocabulary. Afro-
      Cuban poetry, he contends, has taught Spanish how to
      dance. Singles out as illustrations the Afro-Cuban
      poetry of Nicolás Guillén and Marcelino Arozarena but
      focuses as well on tango rhythms in the poetry of the
      Afro-Uruguayan Virginia Brindis de Salas.

143. Johnson, Lemuel. "Cross and Consciousness: The Failure
      of Orthodoxy in African and Afro-Hispanic Literature."
      Studies in Afro-Hispanic Literature. Vol. II. Edited
      by Clementine Rabassa and Gladys Seda-Rodríguez.
      Forthcoming.

      Argues that Afro-Hispanic literature shows evidence
      of the failure of Christianity in the black diaspora.
      Contends that such black characters as Máximo in Manuel
      Zapata Olivella's Afro-Colombian novel *Corral de negros*
      (1963), Pedro Marasma in *Nochebuena negra* (1943), the
      Afro-Venezuelan novel of Juan Pablo Sojo, and Asención
      Lastre in Adalberto Ortiz's Afro-Ecuadorian novel
      Juyungo (1943) all share this consciousness of failure
      of orthodox religion.

144. López Morales, Humberto. "Observaciones fonéticas sobre
      la lengua de la poesía afrocubana." *Estudios sobre
      el español de Cuba.* Long Island City: Las Américas
      Publishing Co., 1971, pp. 106-113.

      Writes that the title of Guillén's book *Sóngoro
      cosongo* is a good example of the *jitanjáfora* which is
      responsible for much of the rhythmic musicality typical
      of black poetry. Argues, however, that the linguistic
      peculiarities of black poetry are not original to the
      black race. Many of them--alliteration and onomatopoeia,
      for example--are common, he says, in Western poetic
      tradition.

145. López Tamés, Ramón. "La soledad de las razas." *La narrativa actual de Colombia y su contexto social.* Valladolid: Universidad de Valladolid, 1975, pp. 64-103.

Discusses Colombia's brand of racism particularly in the interior, which he characterizes as not too blatant. Surveys the novels of Arnoldo Palacios and Manuel Zapata Olivella in that context.

146. Madrid-Malo, Nestor. "Estado actual de la novela en Colombia." *Revista interamericana de bibliografía,* 17 (1967), 68-82.

Considers *En Chimá nace un santo* (1963) Zapata Olivella's best work together with *La calle 10* (1960) and *Detrás del rostro* (1963). Affirms that the three taken together show a gradual maturity in style and technique. Writes also that Arnoldo Palacios' *Las estrellas son negras* is one of the best of the novels that appeared in Colombia in the 1940's.

147. Mansour, Mónica. "Circunstancia e imágenes de la poesía negrista." *Revista de la Universidad de México,* 25 (1970), 25-32.

Studies the negristic emphasis on the sexuality of the black and the mulatto woman reflected in the poet's choice of images. Argues that this emphasis leads to the "mulattization" of nature and musical instruments in the work of Nicolás Guillén and others.

148. ———. "El negro en la poesía negrista." *Revista de bellas artes,* no. 33 (1970), 64-70.

Believes discrimination in Latin America was not as extreme as in the English and French colonies. Argues that black poetry grew out of the integrative nature of Cuban society and that Guillén's poetry represents the transformation of *negrismo* to *latinoamericanismo.*

149. Matheus, John F. "African Footprints in Hispanic-American Literature." *Journal of Negro History,* 23 (1938), 265-289.

Surveys the black presence in Hispanic-American literature including one of Ballagas' anthologies of black poetry that contains poems by Cubans of African descent. Underscores the importance of Plácido in the literary history of Spanish America.

150. Mondéjar, Publio L. "Negritud y poesía." *Revista
      nacional de cultura*, no. 204 (1972), 22-33.

      Sees negritude as a legitimate rebellion against
      white racism and an ardent search for black identity.
      Affirms that it is a poetry where slavery, as in the
      works of Nicolás Guillén, is remembered.

151. Montoya Toro, Jorge. "Meridiano de la poesía negra."
      Universidad de Antioquia, no. 10 (1943), 171-180.

      Argues that such black poets in Latin America as
      Nicolás Guillén and Jorge Artel are more seduced by
      rhythm and color than concerned with black suffering.

152. Moore, Gerald. "Introduction." *Seven African Writers*.
      London-Nairobi: Oxford University Press, 1966, pp.
      vii-xx.

      Introduces the volume by arguing that the opening shots
      in the campaign to create a new African literature were
      fired not by Africans but by black writers from the
      Caribbean, where a "genuine alienation" is seen in the
      works of such poets as Nicolás Guillén.

153. Moreno Fraginals, Manuel. "El problema negro en la
      poesía cubana." *Cuadernos hispanoamericanos*, 3 (1948),
      519-530.

      Considers Manzano and Plácido to be natural products
      of a slave society that prevents free expression and
      protest. Believes Plácido would have been shot earlier
      had he expressed more openly the objections he later
      managed to raise. Other black poets wrote during that
      period but less successfully, under the circumstances,
      since Blacks, he says, were brought to cut cane and not
      to write verse. Concludes that the Black in Cuba has
      finally arrived, an arrival symbolically expressed in
      the poetry of Nicolás Guillén.

154. Morris, Robert J., and Lee A. Daniel. "The Black in
      the Hispanic American Theater." *The American Hispanist*,
      7 (1976), 4-6.

      Traces the upswing of interest in the Black and his
      Afro-Hispanic heritage in the literature of the area
      but notes the lack of research on the Black in the His-
      panic American theater. Intends this survey, which
      makes reference to Nicomedes and Victoria Santa Cruz in
      Peru, to be the first attempt to take inventory of this
      theme.

155. Noble, Enrique. "Aspectos étnicos y sociales de la
poesía mulata latinoamericana." *Revista bimestre
cubana*, 74 (1958), 166-179.

Argues for an ethnic-aesthetic interpretation of negristic literature. Sees black (mulatto) poetry as a
symbolic synthesis of the pathos and ethos of the ethnic
groups among whom it is produced. Considers the mulatto
theme to be one of the most interesting and compares
poems on this theme by Nicolás Guillén and Langston
Hughes that are similar and yet completely different because of the different cultural milieu.

156. Ojo-Ade, Femi. "De origen africano, soy cubano: African
Elements in the Literature of Cuba." *African Litera-
ture Today: Africa, America and the Caribbean.* New
York: Africana Publishing Co., 1978, pp. 47-57.

Contends that the black contribution in Cuba, particularly the Yoruba, is obvious despite nationalistic attempts to play it down. Argues also that African oral
literature has greatly influenced all the literature of
Cuba and that the "African type of writing" existed before the advent of the negristic poets in the 1920's
and the 1930's. Declares that Nicolás Guillén is, perhaps, the most important writer in Cuba today but that
Marcelino Arozarena shows an even more profound knowledge of African culture.

157. Olchyk, Martha K. "Historical Approach to Afro-Cuban
Poetry." Ph.D. dissertation, Texas Christian University, 1972. 274pp.

Charges that Nicolás Guillén's poetry has become a
tool of the new Communist government in Cuba and that
Regino Pedroso's humanitarian impulse led him away from
political propaganda. Considers the principal features
of Afro-Cuban poetry to be sensuality, atavistic African-
ism, and social content.

158. Ortiz, Adalberto. "La negritude en la cultura latinoamericana." *Expresiones culturales del Ecuador*, no.
1 (1972), 23-39. Also published in English as "Negritude in Latin American Culture," translated by Miriam
DeCosta. *Blacks in Hispanic Literature: Critical
Essays.* Edited by Miriam DeCosta (see No. 35), pp.
74-82.

Argues that Blacks brought much to the New World, including folktales. Sees negritude as a means of ex-

pression and affirmation and not an end in itself. Defines it as a process of ethnic and cultural fusion on
this continent and not as a "return to Africa" or as an
exaggerated defense of African culture. Recalls from
childhood the Esmeraldas atmosphere that was to mold and
shape his own black literature of later years when he
and Nelson Estupiñán Bass began to write negristic literature in the 1930's and black literature in the 1940's.
Reviews briefly other Ecuadorian writers who have written
on black themes and closes with more detailed commentary
on those works of his that relate to negritude. Does
not comment on his other work, which he classifies as
manifestations of white Western literature.

159. Ortiz, Fernando. "Más acerca de la poesía mulata.
      Escorzos para su estudio." *Revista bimestre cubana*,
      37 (1936), 23-39; 37 (1936), 218-227; 37 (1936), 439-
      443. Reprinted in *Iniciación a la poesía afroameri-
      cana*. Edited by Oscar Fernández de la Vega and Al-
      berto Pamies (see No. 38), pp. 172-202.

Affirms that some black poetry is black or mulatto in
theme but white in language. Illustrates this with
examples from the work of Nicolás Guillén and Regino
Pedroso.

160. ————. "La religión en la poesía mulata." *Estudios
      afrocubanos*, 1 (1937), 15-62.

Identifies Guillén's "Sensemayá" and "Balada del
Güije" as two of the best exponents of African ritual
religion in Cuban poetry. Contrasts Plácido's use of
conventional white religion, and compares these two
poets to Regino Pedroso's social application of religion.

161. Pagés Larraya, Antonio. "Poesía negra del Caribe his-
      panoamericano." *Libro de homenaje a Luis Alberto
      Sánchez, en los 40 años de su docencia universitaria*.
      Lima: [Universidad Mayor Nacional de San Marcos], 1967
      [for 1968], pp. 389-421.

Compares Langston Hughes and Nicolás Guillén. Says
that the former writes a heated poetry full of shouts
and tremors which Hughes feels on behalf of his race.
The latter, on the other hand, does not shout but writes
cordial *sones*, sad at times but happy as well. Guillén's
song, he affirms, is that of a man who has suffered injustices but who, nevertheless, feels himself a part of
his environment. Mentions Plácido briefly and charac-

terizes Pedroso and Guillén as militant Communists.
Argues that such black poets as Plácido and Guillén
counsel Blacks to accept their origins.

162. Pedersen, Carl E., Jr. "Main Trends in the Contemporary
Colombian Novel, 1953-1967." Ph.D. dissertation,
University of Southern California, 1971. 412pp.

Places the black novel of Arnoldo Palacios and Manuel
Zapata Olivella within main trends in the Colombian
novel since 1953 but identifies Palacios' novel *Las
estrellas son negras*, published in 1949, as the best
naturalistic novel in Colombia. Says that Manuel Zapata
Olivella has dedicated himself to *literatura comprometida*
but not always with much success artistically. Sees an
early influence of social realism in Zapata Olivella's
first novel *Tierra mojada* and says his *En Chimá nace un
santo* represents the high point of the novelistic art
of an author who imbues most of his works with revolu-
ionary social protest, especially in *Corral de negros*.

163. Peña, Pedro J. de la. "Tres calas en la poesía negra."
Atlántida (1971), 798-809.

Divides black poetry into three categories: Sub-Sa-
haran, Afro-American (including such countries as Brazil,
Cuba, Haiti, and the United States), and European,
written by Africans settled in Paris, Brussels, and
London. Argues that there is also African poetry written
by Whites settled in Rhodesia, for example, and in South
Africa. Argues as well that Nicolás Guillén is a cultured poet of the people, one adept in oral stylistic
means and superior because of his New World experiences
and his talent.

164. Pereda Valdés, Ildefonso. "El negro en la literatura
iberoamericana." *Cuadernos*, 19 (1956), 104-110.

States that the poetry of Nicolás Guillén passes
through all of the stages that "mulatto" poetry went
through. Applies criteria, developed by Fernando Ortiz,
to the Afro-Uruguayan poetry of Pilar Barrios and Julio
Arrascaeta. Classifies black poetry thematically into
three categories, namely, universal themes, social
themes (slavery and racial discrimination), and *mulatez*,
and sees key aspects to be plasticity, ritual, super-
stition, sensuality, onomatopoeia, and rhythm.

165. Pereza, Luis. "El indio y el negro en nuestro teatro."
El farol (Caracas) (1946), 2.

Disagrees with those who think Venezuela, because it
has Blacks, Indians, and Mestizoes, is incapable of
having a national theater. Points to Juan Pablo Sojo
as the initiator of black theater in the country.

166. Portuondo, José Antonio. "El negro, héroe, bufón y
persona en la literatura cubana colonial (1608-1896)."
Etnología y folklore, no. 7 (1969), 63-68. Also in
Unión, 6 (1968), 30-36.

Sees Manzano and Plácido as victims but heroic ones.
Argues that the Black as person culminates in the work
of Martín Morúa Delgado, whose novels are not just novels
on black themes but novels written from a black perspective where human dignity is the central core.

167. ———. "Las masas." *El contenido social de la literatura cubana*. Mexico: El Colegio de México, 1944, pp.
71-86. Reprinted in *Bosquejo histórico de las letras
cubanas*. Havana: Ministerio de Relaciones Exteriores,
1960, pp. 41-69.

States that the *negrista* movement in Cuba is the Cuban
version of the *indigenismo* taking place elsewhere in
Iberoamerica. Highlights the protest element of Nicolás Guillén's poetry which stands out against the more
picturesque poetry practiced by other *negrista* poets,
thanks in part, he says, to the influence of Langston
Hughes. Also discusses the early proletarian protest
poetry of Regino Pedroso.

168. Revuelta, Manuel. "La poesía negra." *Poesía hispanoamericana de hoy*. Valladolid: Sever Cuesta, 1967,
pp. 34-36.

169. Ribandeneira M., Edmundo. "La presencia del negro."
La moderna novela ecuatoriana. Quito: Editorial Casa
de la Cultura Ecuatoriana, 1958, pp. 136-138.

Considers Adalberto Ortiz's *Juyungo* to be the first
black novel in Ecuador and Nelson Estupiñán Bass's
Cuando los guayacanes florecían the second.

170. Rodríguez Embril, Luis. *La poesía negra en Cuba*.
Santiago: Universidad de Chile, 1939. 16pp.

Argues in this article that early black poets in Latin
America, unlike black poets in this century, were black
only in color. Contends that their works, as in the
cases of Manzano and Plácido, were imitations of poetry
of white Spanish poets.

171. Romero, Fernando. "Los estudios afrocubanos y el negro
    en la patria de Martí." *Revista bimestre cubana*, 47
    (1941), 395-401.

    Primarily discusses Fernando Ortiz's article "La reli-
    gión en la poesía mulata." Focuses on such black poets
    as Plácido who, out of a desire to compete on white
    terms, lose contact with African religious themes.

172. Schons, Dorothy. "Negro poetry in the Americas."
    Hispania, 14 (1942), 309-319.

    Affirms that Latin American black verse is based on
    African cults and that there is nothing comparable in
    Latin America to the North American spirituals. Asserts
    also that the Latin American Black's "love of rhythm"
    finds expression in song and dance rhythms that have
    been much used by such poets as Nicolás Guillén. The
    strongest bond between black poets in the United States
    and in Latin America lies, she contends, in the theme
    of racial protest.

173. Smart, Ian. "Some Thoughts on the African Contribution
    to Spanish American Literature." *Ufahamu*, 7 (1977),
    73-91.

    Gives a panoramic view of the black theme in Spanish
    American literature while describing negritude in that
    part of the world. Discusses the white verse and Euro-
    pean standards followed by such early black writers as
    Plácido and Manzano. Calls Ortiz's *Juyungo* the most
    significant Afro-Antillean novel, and affirms that if
    there is a Spanish American negritude the best example
    of it would be found in the works of Nicolás Guillén,
    whose *son* poems represent the beginning of the poet's
    greatness. Concludes that the sense of honest identi-
    fication felt by such poets as Regino Pedroso, Nicolás
    Guillén, and Marcelino Arozarena is a necessary prere-
    quisite for any truly authentic expression of the Afri-
    can heritage. Contends, however, that Guillén's posi-
    tion as a poet of synthesis is one that goes beyond
    negritude, or perhaps betrays it.

174. Spratlin, Valaurez. "The Negro in Spanish Literature."
    Journal of Negro History, 10 (1934), 62-71. Reprinted
    in *Blacks in Hispanic Literature: Critical Essays*.
    Edited by Miriam DeCosta (see No. 35), pp. 47-52.

Itemizes the black presence in Spanish literature but turns midway from Spain to the black presence in Spanish American history and literature. Does not go into detail on Manzano and Plácido, but believes that stark realism makes Manzano's autobiography a more remarkable document than *Uncle Tom's Cabin* and that Plácido's fate was even more tragic than Manzano's.

175. Stimson, Frederick S. "Poesía negra: Nicolás Guillén (Cuba)." *The New Schools of Spanish American Poetry.* Chapel Hill: University of North Carolina, 1970, pp. 161-179.

Reviews the Negrophilism of the early 1920's--its causes, role, and achievement--as an important aspect of the European Vanguard movement in literature and art. Sees Cuba as the leading center for the cultivation of black poetry in America whose leading exponent was the "famous" Nicolás Guillén. The work of this poet, he argues, shows the themes and such stylistic peculiarities characteristic of black poetry as beat, onomatopoeia, and use of the *jitanjáfora*.

176. Suárez-Murias, Margarite C. "Interdisciplinary Credit in the Humanities: Black Literature in Latin America in Translation." *Latin American Literary Review*, 4 (1975), 49-56.

Calls for more interdisciplinary courses not on black authors but on black literature, which she defines as "that aspect of the Belles Lettres which deals with the subject of Black people, individually or collectively, as depicted by any author of merit irrespective of his ancestry."

177. Suárez Radillo, Carlos Miguel. "El negro y su encuentro de sí mismo a través teatro." *Cuadernos hispanoamericanos*, 91 (1973), 34-40.

Considers *mestizaje* to be an unmistakable sign of Latin American racial composition. Argues, however, that the Black has imposed his influence and that there exist in America artistic means of expression that are authentically black, and not just in music and in dance but in theater as well. Prefers to see theater where Blacks and Whites can play roles with no regard for color, but recognizes the impossibility of this at the present time. Concentrates on the black dance company of Victoria Santa Cruz, who rejects the white aesthetic and identifies more with Blacks, as she considers such identification the first step toward mestizo, Peruvian, and universal expression.

178. Torre, Guillermo de. "Literatura de color." *Revista bimestre cubana*, 38 (1936), 5-11. Also in *La aventura y el orden*. Buenos Aires, 1943, pp. 305-314.

Contends that the origin of *negrismo* lies in Cubism and in Europe shortly after the turn of the century but that Cuba is the source of considerable black poetry. Does not see much elsewhere in Spanish America. Characterizes black expression as childlike, charming, and happy.

179. Torres-Rioseco, Arturo. "Negro Verse." *The Epic of Latin American Literature*. Berkeley and Los Angeles: University of California Press, 1942. New printing, 1959, pp. 127-132.

One of the first to see black poetry as an emerging and highly original genre with a "beat" not based on Spanish versification. One of the first also to identify Nicolás Guillén as a classic poet and to classify him as one of the best exponents of this genre. Asserts that Guillén's art goes beyond racial differences and national boundaries. Also considers Marcelino Arozarena to be the author of inspired black poetry.

180. Valbuena Briones, Angel. "El tema negro en la poesía antillana." *Literatura hispanoamericana*. Barcelona: Gustavo Gili, 1962, pp. 413-431.

Sees close similarity between treatment of the Black in Golden Age literature and in contemporary black poetry. Says first conscious products of this literary current are found in Modernism but that Cuba became the artistic capital with Nicolás Guillén—perhaps under García Lorca's influence—its most representative poet.

181. Valdés-Cruz, Rosa E. "Tres poemas representativos de la poesía afro-antillana." *Hispania*, 54 (1971), 39-45.

Points out basic thematic motifs of Afro-Antillean poetry but contends that racial and social themes with the exception of Nicolás Guillén's poetry are more prominent in English and French America. Includes analysis of one poem of Nicolás Guillén to illustrate the theme of social injustice.

182. Varela, José Luis. "La poesía mulata." *Ensayos de
      poesía indígena en Cuba.* Madrid: Cultura Hispánica,
      1951, pp. 75-120.

183. Vitier, Cintio. "Dos poetas cubanos, Plácido y Manzano."
      Bohemia (December 14, 1973), pp. 19-21.

      Emphasizes the poetic force incorrect spelling can
      have in literary expression. Uses César Vallejo's
      poetry and Manzano's *Autobiografía* as examples. Clari-
      fies that Manzano stopped writing not after gaining his
      freedom but after the government purge following the
      Conspiración de la Escalera. Argues that Manzano had
      more direct exposure than Plácido to the evils of a
      slave society. Contends also that Plácido's poetic
      talent was greater than Manzano's but that the latter's
      poetry was more "deep" and less superficial.

184. Walker, Michael Lee. "The Black Social Identity in
      Selected Novels of Nelson Estupiñán Bass and Adalberto
      Ortiz." Ph.D. dissertation, University of California,
      Riverside, 1977. 194pp.

      Examines *El último río* by Nelson Estupiñán Bass and
      Juyungo by Adalberto Ortiz "to determine the extent to
      which the two black Ecuadorian writers believe in the
      existence of a racial democracy in Ecuador and Spanish
      America as a whole." Concludes that the black Ecuador-
      ians in these novels suffer because of their color,
      their culture, and their socio-economic class. Includes
      an interview with the two writers.

185. Williams, Lorna. "Pan-Africanism and Latin American
      Literature." *Issue. Africa 2000.* In press.

186. ―――. "The Black Woman and Revolution in Cuba."
      Revista/Review Interamericana. In press.

      Sees a "diffuseness of focus" in recent Cuban litera-
      ture dealing with black women and revolutionary con-
      sciousness. Illustrates this point with examples rang-
      ing from the "disoriented vision" Severo Sarduy gives
      the black woman in *Gestos* and the "collective vision"
      given her by Nancy Morejón in her poem "mujer negra"
      to the "superior moral vision" Nicolás Guillén gives
      her in his poem "Angela Davis."

187. Wilson, Carlos. "Aspectos de la prosa narrativa pana-
      meña contemporánea." Ph.D. dissertation, University
      of California, Los Angeles, 1975. 218pp.

Contains a chapter on the Black in Panamanian literature. Reviews racist practices in the country that are
reflected in the literature. Identifies Rogelio Sinán
and Joaquín Beleño C. as the two Panamanian writers who
have dealt most with the black theme. Earlier black
Panamanian poets, he says, tried hard to avoid it.

188. Wilson, Leslie N. "El negro en la poesía hispanoamericana." *College Language Association Journal*, 13
(1970), 335-349. Also published in English as "*La
poesía negra*: Its Background, Themes and Significance."
Translated by Leslie N. Wilson. *Blacks in Hispanic
Literature: Critical Essays*. Edited by Miriam DeCosta
(see No. 35), pp. 90-104.

Argues that Afro-Antillean poetry is as important a
New World creation as *poesía gauchesca*, as poetry on
the Indian, or any other kind; that black poetry by
Whites is hypocritical in that Whites want to speak for
Blacks without sincerely feeling or understanding black
suffering; that the name "social poetry" characterizes
black poetry very well; that Nicolás Guillén is the
leading poet in this movement; and that the *jitanjáfora*
is one of black poetry's most distinctive elements.

189. Young, Ann Ventura. "The Black Woman in Afro-Caribbean
Poetry." *Blacks in Hispanic Literature: Critical
Essays*. Edited by Miriam DeCosta (see No. 35), pp.
137-142.

Illustrates that the Afro-Cuban poets Marcelino Arozarena and Nicolás Guillén, unlike white poets who cultivate black poetry, do not limit their portrayal of
the Afro-American woman to a one-dimensional characterization of her as a primitive sensual creature.

190. Zea, Leopoldo. "Negritud e indigenismo." *Cuadernos
americanos*, 197 (1974), 16-30.

Sees negritude and indigenism as reactions against
the dependency syndrome imposed by racial and cultural
superiority emanating from Europe, with the distinction
that negritude arises from the black man himself while
indigenism arises from nonindigenous defenders of the
Indian.

III

AUTHORS AND CRITICISM

AROZARENA, MARCELINO   (Cuba, 1912-   )

A. Works

191.   *Canción negra sin color.*   Havana: Ediciones Unión, 1966.
       71pp.   Reprint.   Nendeln: Kraus, 1970.

       Contains Arozarena's poems, which he had published
       separately since the 1930's.

B. Criticism

192.   DeCosta Willis, Miriam.   "Arozarena's *Black Song.*"
       Revista/Review Interamericana, 6 (1976), 349-355.

       Contends that Arozarena has not received the critical
       attention his poetry deserves.   Attributes this neglect
       partly to his political views and close association
       with Communist leaders.   Analyzes the poet's style and
       thematic content, which she sees as essentially militant
       and revolutionary.

See also Nos. 17, 26, 47, 48, 62, 85, 86, 100, 109, 135, 142,
156, 173, 179, 189.

ARTEL, JORGE `(Colombia, 1909-   )

A. Works

193.   *Tambores en la noche.*   Bogotá: Ediciones Bolívar, 1940.
       Reprint.   Guanajuato: Ediciones de la Universidad de
       Guanajuato, 1955.

       One of the several books of *black* poetry published in
       the 1940's by black authors in Spanish America.

B. Criticism

194. Caneva, Rafael. "Jorge Artel." *Universidad de Antio-
     quia* (Medellin), 1 (1945), 89-95.

     Asserts that Artel writes poetry reminiscent of the
     sensual *cumbia*. Does not believe that Artel has much
     in common with Candelario Obeso. Sees Artel's poetry
     as thoroughly black, complete with race pride, concern
     for the hardships of his black brothers, and awareness
     of their happier moments.

194a. Prescott, Lawrence E. "Jorge Artel y sus tambores en
      la noche." *Diario del Caribe* (Barranquilla) (October
      5, 1975), 1, 4-5.

      Defends Artel against charges that he does not write
      black poetry. Argues that the author of *Tambores en la
      noche* is "the black poet of Colombia" and that the black
      poems in this book, especially in the 1955 edition, are
      of a very high quality. Classifies Artel's poetry into
      three recognized categories of black poetry, namely,
      descriptive, popular or folkloric, and social or poli-
      tical.

See also Nos. 12, 17, 151.

BARRIOS, PILAR (Uruguay, 1889-)

A. Works

195. *Piel negra. Poesías (1917-1947).* Montevideo: Nuestra
     Raza, 1947. 113pp. Reprint. Nendeln: Kraus, 1970.

     This book, Barrios' first, together with his other
     two listed below, is available in one volume in the
     Kraus reprint.

196. *Mis cantos.* Montevideo: Comité Amigos del poeta, 1949.
     132pp. Reprint. Nendeln: Kraus, 1970.

197. *Campo afuera.* Montevideo: Publicaciones Minerva, 1959.
     79pp. Reprint. Nendeln: Kraus, 1970.

     A volume of poetry highlighted by Barrios' skillful
     use of gaucho dialect.

B. Criticism

198. Britos, Alberto. "Prólogo." *Piel negra*. Montevideo: Nuestra Raza, 1947, pp. 9-15.

Reviews the Black and his culture in Uruguay. Discusses the biography of the poet, and the themes of his poetry, which he characterizes as romantic, melancholic, tender, musical, and especially strong on the exaltation of black motherhood and black liberation.

See also Nos. 59, 60, 98, 164.

BRINDIS DE SALAS, VIRGINIA   (Uruguay)

A. Works

199. *Pregón de marimorena*. Montevideo: Sociedad Cultural Editora Indoamericana, 1946.   59pp.

200. *Cien cárceles de amor*. Montevideo, 1949.   45pp.

B. Criticism

201. Guadalupe, Julio. "Virginia Brindis de Salas y su poesía realista." "Prólogo." In Virginia Brindis de Salas. *Pregón de marimorena* (see No. 199), pp. 7-14.

Considers black pride to be strong in Uruguay with Brindis de Salas' work contributing to it. Does not see any "art for art's sake" emphasis in her poetry but recognizes in it a revolutionary sense enriched by a popular flavor she takes from and returns to her audience.

202. Jackson, Richard L. "*Nuestra raza*, Black Literary Expression and the Afro-Uruguayan Poetry of Virginia Brindis de Salas." Originally scheduled for publication in *Latin American Literary Review*; this has been withdrawn but will appear, in part, in Richard L. Jackson's *Black Writers in Latin America* (see No. 46).

Argues that women writers, particularly Virginia Brindis de Salas, were distinguished contributors to black literary journals in Uruguay. Contends that Brindis de Salas' poetry can serve as a thematic model for black literary expression in Spanish America since her poems develop the identification with blackness, the rejection of white racism, and the emphasis on universal solidarity now recognized as central themes of negritude.

See also Nos. 49, 59, 142.

DUNCAN, QUINCE   (Costa Rica, 1940-   )

A. Works

203. *El pozo y una carta*. San José: Cuadernos de Arte Popular, 1969.

204. *Bronce*. San José: Cuadernos de Arte Popular, 1970.

205. *Una canción en la madrugada*. San José: Editorial Costa Rica, 1970. 81pp.

206. *Mangonia y otras yeguadas*. San José: Cuadernos de Arte Popular, 1971.   .

207. *Hombres curtidos*. San José: Editorial Territorio, 1971. 141pp.

   Duncan's first novel.

208. *El negro en Costa Rica*. San José: Editorial Costa Rica, 1972.   281pp.

   An anthology of essays and articles, two of them by Carlos Meléndez, who co-edited the volume.

209. *Los cuatro espejos*. San José: Editorial Costa Rica, 1973.   165pp.

   Duncan's most ambitious psychological novel, recipient of an "Honorable Mention" in a recent novel competition in Costa Rica.

210. *Los cuentos del Hermano Araña*. San José: Editorial Territorio, 1975.

211. *El negro en la literatura costarricense*. San José: Editorial Costa Rica, 1975.   191pp.

   A prologue by Fabián Doblés and an introduction by Duncan head up this anthology in which Duncan's own work is amply represented.

B. Criticism

212. Chase, Alfonso, ed. "Quince Duncan (1940)." *Narrativa
     contemporánea de Costa Rica*. 2 vols. San José: Mini-
     sterio de Cultura, Juventud y Deportes, 1975. Vol. II,
     pp. 333-353.

     An anthology that includes short stories of Quince
     Duncan. Volume I leads off with a comprehensive intro-
     duction called "Notes for a History of the Contemporary
     Narrative" of Costa Rica. Volume II includes an up-to-
     date bibliography of Duncan's works and studies about
     him.

213. Sánchez M., Alvaro. "El negro en la literatura costar-
     ricense." *El negro en Costa Rica*. Edited by Quince
     Duncan and Carlos Meléndez (see No. 208), pp. 161-175.

     Largely a review of the black theme in the literature
     of Costa Rica as developed by nonblack writers but closes
     with a brief mention of Quince Duncan and two of his
     books.

ESTUPINAN BASS, NELSON (Ecuador, 1915-   )

A. Works

214. *Cuando los guayacanes florecían*. Quito: Casa de la
     Cultura Ecuatoriana, 1954. 307pp.

215. *Canto negro por la luz. Poemas para negros y blancos*.
     Esmeraldas: Ediciones del Núcleo Provincial de Esmer-
     aldas de la Casa de la Cultura Ecuatoriana, 1954.
     83pp.

216. *Timarán y Cuabú: cuaderno de poesía para el pueblo*.
     Quito: Casa de la Cultura Ecuatoriana, 1956. 93pp.

     In this volume Estupiñán Bass continues to vary his
     medium: his first book was a novel, his second a collec-
     tion of highly sophisticated verse, and this, his third,
     a book of popular poetry written in *copla* form.

217. *El paraíso*. Quito: Casa de la Cultura Ecuatoriana,
     1958. 319pp.

218. *El último río*. Quito: Casa de la Cultura Ecuatoriana,
     1967. 267pp.

219. *Las huellas digitales.* Quito: Casa de la Cultura Ecua-
     toriana, 1971. 57pp.

220. *Las tres carabelas.* Porto Viejo: Editorial Gregorio,
     1973.

     Unlike Estupiñán Bass's other books, this one is a
     mixed collection of poetry, stories, and plays.

221. *Senderos brillantes.* Quito: Casa de la Cultura Ecuatori-
     ana, 1974. 300pp.

     The first of three recent novels by Nelson Estupiñán
     Bass that are experimental in form and technique.

222. *Las puertas del verano.* Quito: Editorial Casa de la
     Cultura Ecuatoriana, 1978. 273pp.

223. *Toque de queda.* Guayaquil: Casa de la Cultura Ecuatori-
     ana, Núcleo del Guayas, 1978. 120pp.

224. *El desempate. 2º cuaderno de poesía para el pueblo.*
     Forthcoming.

     A sequel to *Timarán y Cuabú*, with the two popular
     singers continuing their verbal duel.

B. Criticism

225. Jackson, Richard L. "La novelística de Nelson Estupiñán
     Bass." *El comercio* (September 24, 1978), 3.

     Focuses on *Toque de queda.* Argues that this novel,
     like Estupiñán Bass's *Las puertas del verano* and *Senderos
     brillantes*, his other two recent novels, rejects tra-
     ditional novelistic techniques. Concludes that these
     three novels signal the author's adoption of a new ar-
     tistic vision but one that does not abandon his social
     and political concerns.

226. ———. "Nelson Estupiñán Bass' *Senderos brillantes.*"
     Inter-American Review of Bibliography, 27 (1977),
     76-78.

     Contends that concepts of Third World consciousness
     as well as concepts of literary blackness can be applied
     to *Senderos brillantes.* Argues that in this novel na-
     tional identity becomes an ultimate question as does
     confrontation, not just with racist Whites but with neo-
     colonialist forces of imperialism as well.

227. Martán Góngora, Helcias. "Nelson Estupiñán: *El último río.*" *Boletín cultural y bibliográfico*, 10 (1967), 356-357.

Reviews the author's status as a cultured poet but one who also writes popular poetry and novels. Considers a racial complex to be the main protagonist of *El último río*, particularly as reflected in the role of Pastrana, a character reminiscent, he thinks, of Eugene O'Neill's Emperor Jones.

228. Rengel, Jorge Hugo. "Nelson Estupiñán Bass y la poesía negra ecuatoriana." Nelson Estupiñán Bass. *Canto negro por la luz* (see No. 215), pp. 7-17.

Recalls Paul Valéry and Pablo Neruda, among others, in his discussion of Estupiñán Bass's poetry. Says that nature and the black woman are thematic constants in his poetry, which is noted for its free verse style. Sees Estupiñán Bass as a revolutionary.

229. Tinajero Villamar, Fernando. "Una historia de pasión." In Nelson Estupiñán Bass. *El último río* (see No. 218), pp. 9-14.

Gives *El último río* a political interpretation, seeing in the impotence and failure of Pastrana, the protagonist, the failure of an old and worn out liberalism in Ecuador.

See also Nos. 36, 158, 169, 184.

GUILLEN, NICOLAS (Cuba, 1902-)

A. Works

230. *Motivos de son.* Havana: Rambla y Bouza, 1930. 12pp.

231. *Sóngoro cosongo (poemas mulatos).* Havana: Ucar y García y Cía., 1931. 56pp.

232. *West Indies Ltd.* Havana: Ucar y García y Cía., 1934. 48pp.

233. *Cantos para soldados y sones para turistas.* Mexico: Editorial Masas, 1937. 84pp.

234. *España: poema en cuatro angustias y una esperanza.* Mexico: Editorial México Nuevo, 1937. 26pp.

235. *Sóngoro cosongo y otros poemas*. Havana: Editorial La
      Verónica, 1942. 120pp.

236. *El son entero; suma poética, 1929-1946*. Buenos Aires:
      Editorial Pleamar, 1947. 210pp.

237. *Elegía a Jacques Roumain en el cielo de Haití*. Havana:
      Impr. Ayón, 1948. 15pp.

238. *Cuba libre*. Translated by Langston Hughes and Ben
      Frederic Carruthers. Los Angeles: The Ward Ritchie
      Press, 1948. 98pp.

239. *Elegía a Jesús Menéndez*. Havana: Páginas, 1951. 51pp.

240. *La paloma de vuelo polular, elegías*. Buenos Aires:
      Editorial Losada, 1958. 157pp.

241. *Prosa de prisa: crónicas*. Santa Clara: Universidad
      Central de Las Villas, 1962. 343pp.

242. *Antología mayor*. Havana: Bolsilibros Unión, 1964.
      284pp.

243. *Poemas de amor*. Havana: La Tertulia, 1964. 57pp.

244. *Tengo*. Havana: Universidad Central de Las Villas, 1964.
      197pp.

245. *El Gran Zoo*. Madrid: Editorial Ciencia Nueva, 1969.
      71pp.

246. *Antología clave*. Edited by Luis Iñigo Madrigal.
      Santiago de Chile: Editorial Nascimento, 1971. 194pp.

247. *El diario que a diario*. Havana: Instituto Cubano del
      Libro, 1972. 87pp.

248. *La rueda dentada*. Havana: Instituto Cubano del Libro,
      1972. 131pp.

249. *Man-Making Words. Selected Poems of Nicolás Guillén*.
      Translated by Robert Márquez and David A. McMurray.
      Amherst: University of Massachusetts Press, 1972.
      214pp.

250. *¡Patria o muerte! The Great Zoo and Other Poems by
      Nicolás Guillén*. Translated by Robert Márquez. New
      York: Monthly Review Press, 1972. 223pp.

251. *Obra poética (1920-1972)*. 2 vols. Havana: Editorial
     Arte y Literatura, 1974. 570pp. 574pp.

252. *Tengo*. Translated by Richard J. Carr. Detroit: Broad-
     side Press, 1974. 142pp.

253. *Summa poética*. Edited by Luis Iñigo Madrigal. Madrid:
     Ediciones Cátedra, 1976. 299pp.

254. *Prosa de prisa 1929-1972*. 3 vols. Havana: Editorial
     Arte y Literatura, 1976. 427pp., 457pp., 442pp.

     B. Criticism

        1. Bibliography

255. Biblioteca Nacional José Martí. *Bibliografía de Nico-
     lás Guillén*. Havana: Instituto Cubano del Libro,
     1975. 379pp.

     A massive bibliography complete with index of titles,
     index of authors, and a list of publications consulted
     to complement the entries on works by or about Guillén
     that make up the volume. The secondary bibliography
     of works on Guillén, which runs through 1972, takes
     up only 59 of the 379 pages while the primary bibliog-
     raphy, which lists his works and translations of them,
     makes up the largest section. Contents of poetry col-
     lections are included and Guillén's works are listed
     chronologically in the order of publication. The same
     order applied to books and articles prevails in the
     listing of criticism.

256. Center for Cuban Studies. "A Short Guillén Bibliog-
     raphy." *Center for Cuban Studies Newsletter*, no. 2
     (1974), 15-18.

     A partial bibliography that lists works primarily
     concerned with Guillén the poet and only those in Span-
     ish or English. Xeroxes sections of the extensive bibliog-
     raphy included in the second volume of Guillén's *Obra
     poética (1920-1972)*. Refers to the more comprehensive
     bibliography recently published in Cuba (see No. 255)
     but does not mention the extremely thorough bibliog-
     raphy included in *Recopilación de textos sobre Nico-
     lás Guillén*, edited by Nancy Morejón (see No. 261).

2. Books

257. Augier, Angel. *Nicolás Guillén, notas para un estudio
      biográfico crítico.* 2 vols. Santa Clara: Universi-
      dad Central de Las Villas, 1962-1964. 237pp., 299pp.
      Published in one abridged volume as *Nicolás Guillén.*
      Havana: Instituto Cubano deĺ Libro, 1971. 318pp.

      Traces Guillén's biography and poetic trajectory up
      to 1934 (*West Indies Ltd.*) in Volume I and to 1948 (*El
      son entero*) in Volume II. Includes press reception of
      Guillén's work and travels around Spanish America. Is
      especially careful to set Guillén's life and work
      against the backdrop of the historical, social, politi-
      cal, and economic conditions of his time. Documents
      this basic biography with photographs.

258. Couffon, Claude, ed. *Nicolás Guillén: Présentation,
      choix de textes, traduction.* Paris: Seghers, 1964.
      191pp.

      Contains long biographical introduction, especially
      concerning Guillén's early years. Includes photographs
      and a broad selection of texts representative of his
      production up to 1963.

259. Fernández Retamar, Roberto. *El son de vuelo popular.*
      Havana: Unión, 1972. 89pp.

      Includes "El son de vuelo popular" and three other
      essays on Guillén. The first essay, "Guillén en la
      poesía contemporánea cubana," traces Guillén's develop-
      ment from black poetry to social poetry. The second
      essay, the shortest in the collection, "Sobre Guillén,
      poeta cubano," classifies Guillén as a national poet in
      whom Africa and Spain are combined. The final essay
      "¿Quién es el autor de la poesía de Nicolás Guillén?"
      answers the question raised in the title by pointing
      to the Cuban people, the source of Guillén's poetic
      inspiration.

260. Martínez Estrada, Ezequiel. *La poesía afro-cubana de
      Nicolás Guillén.* Montevideo: Arca, 1966. 92pp.
      Reprint. Buenos Aires: Calicanto, 1977. 159pp.

      Argues that Guillén's verse, like the poet himself,
      has little to do with Africa; that Guillén is more
      European than African in his tastes, habits, and liter-
      ary preferences; that Guillén's poetry is more social
      than racial; and that it is more to be heard, prefer-

ably as spoken by Guillén himself, than to be read. Concludes that with Guillén we have basically a learned, correct poet who writes an unlettered, incorrect poetry. The 1977 reprint contains an anthology of Guillén's poetry selected by Horacio Salas.

261. Morejón, Nancy, ed. *Recopilación de textos sobre Nicolás Guillén*. Havana: Casa de las Américas, 1974. 429pp.

Designed to present a collection of works that will give a balanced view of Guillén and to correct some misconceptions regarding his poetry. Largely includes, however, works of Cuban authors and foreign Marxists. Introduction to the volume reviews the criticism as well as the works of Guillén with the same intent: to lift Guillén out of the restricted category of writer of black poetry only. Argues in the Introduction that Guillén is the most Spanish of Cuban poets. Concludes that Guillén criticism has been too "black" or impressionistic and too critical of his political stance, that is, too right wing in one direction and too liberal in another.

262. Ruscalleda Bercedoniz, Jorge María. *Cuatro elementos sustanciales en la poesía de Nicolás Guillén*. Río Piedras: Editorial Universitaria, Universidad de Puerto Rico, 1975. 310pp.

Analyzes the poetic output of Nicolás Guillén from his earliest work to his most recent. Claims to build on the work of Angel Augier, Ezequiel Martínez Estrada, Wilfred Cartey, and Rosa E. Valdés-Cruz and does so by examining in detail the themes, techniques, and style of the poet's work, which he believes is a reflection of the time in which it was written. Includes statistical summary of strophes and verse frequency in Guillén's poetry.

263. Sardinha, Dennis. *The Poetry of Nicolás Guillén. An Introduction*. London: New Books Ltd., 1976. 80pp.

An enlarged version of a speech which the author revised to include a chapter on Guillén's style and a translation of an interview with the poet held in 1972. Concludes that stylistically Guillén combines his intimate knowledge of black dialect and rhythm with a desire to break away from the set forms of literature.

264.   Tous, Adriana. *La poesía de Nicolás Guillén*. Madrid:
        Cultura Hispánica, 1971. 161pp.

        Argues that Guillén's primary contributions to black
        poetry lie in his intention to create in the Black a
        sense of pride and to incorporate the *son* into formal
        poetic structure. Believes that the greatest value of
        Guillén's poetry is the inside view it gives of the
        black experience, folklore, and language in Cuba.

265.   Williams, Lorna. *Self and Society in the Poetry of
        Nicolás Guillén*. Baltimore: Johns Hopkins University
        Press [Perhaps to be withdrawn and submitted to an-
        other publisher], forthcoming.

        Examines the dialectical relationship between self and
        other in the work of Nicolás Guillén. Argues that
        Guillén does not see man governed by genetic traits and
        that he does not advocate a "mystical leap across time
        and space into a pristine African culture." Examines
        Guillén's work from an interdisciplinary perspective
        with particular reliance on the theories and observa-
        tions of Franklin W. Knight and Harry Hoetink. Contends
        that self-perception is affected by one's situation
        within one's society and evaluates Guillén's perception
        of his world and how that perception affects his poetry
        about it.

            3. Articles, Shorter Studies, and Dissertations

266.   Aguirre, Mirta. "Guillén, maestro de poesía." *La
        gaceta de Cuba*, 1 (1962), 16-18. Reprinted in *Reco-
        pilación de textos sobre Nicolás Guillén*. Edited by
        Nancy Morejón (see No. 261), pp. 159-170.

        Considers *Motivos de son* and *Sóngoro cosongo* as first
        steps only and *Elegía a Jesús Menéndez* the most beauti-
        ful revolutionary poem ever written in the Spanish
        language. Sees much of Lope de Vega, Góngora, and
        Quevedo in Guillén's poetry.

267.   ————. "En torno a la elegía a Jesús Menéndez." *La
        última hora*, no. 23 (July 10, 1952), 3-4. Reprinted
        in *Recopilación de textos sobre Nicolás Guillén*.
        Edited by Nancy Morejón (see No. 261), pp. 293-302.

        Considers this poem in its orchestration to be the
        equivalent of a revolutionary oratory, a masterfully
        composed poem whose artistry ranges from the simple
        to the complex, from free verse and prose to the set
        forms of literature.

268. Allen, Marta E. "Nicolás Guillén, poeta del pueblo."
      Revista iberoamericana, 15 (1949), 23-43.

      Contends that Guillén is not one of those poets who,
      speaking over the heads of the people, always employ a
      difficult language. Believes his basic themes relate
      to the lives and the daily hard times of the little
      man, an outgrowth of his hope for true brotherhood
      among all men.

269. Antón Quesada, Héctor. "Poesía y música. El ritmo en
      la poesía de Nicolás Guillén." *En busca de la poesía
      pura, esquiscio filosófico-literario*. Havana: Imp.
      Ucar y García y Cía., 1960, pp. 26-30.

      Affirms that Guillén's poetry reveals the "natural
      instinct" that Blacks have for rhythm and music and that
      "Balada del güije" and "Sensemayá" are the best illus-
      trations of this trait.

270. Arozarena, Marcelino. "El antillano domador de sones."
      Revista América, 17 (1943), 37-42.

271. Augier, Angel. "Alusiones afrocubanas en la poesía de
      Nicolás Guillén." *Unión*, 6 (1969), 143-151. Re-
      printed in *Etnología y folklore*, no. 7 (1969), 69-74.

      Contends that the African presence in Guillén's early
      poems manifested itself polemically through social pro-
      test. Believes his fighting spirit becomes more lyri-
      cal in later years, a transformation of sentiment he
      ascribes to transculturation.

272. ————. "La afirmación revolucionaria de las Elegías."
      Bohemia, no. 29 (July 21, 1972), 46-53.

      Reveals that *Las elegías elegidas*--an alliteration
      reminiscent of Guillén's *Prosa de prisa*--was one of the
      possible titles the poet considered for his collection
      of elegies. Asserts that the six elegies are dissimilar
      in subject matter but that they all fit into a progres-
      sive movement of the poet from his personal-based "El
      apellido" to the continental dimensions of his "Elegía
      a Jesús Menéndez." Nevertheless, considers his
      "Elegía camagüeyana"--with its autobiographical ele-
      ments--to be Guillén's most personal one.

273. ————. "La crítica extranjera ante la obra de Nico-
      lás Guillén." *La gaceta de Cuba*, 1 (1962), 4-6.

Says that such Cuban critics as himself, Juan Marinello, Jorge Manach, Regino Boti, José Antonio Portuondo, Cintio Vitier, and Roberto Fernández Retamar recognize the exceptional value of Guillén's poetry and that such foreign critics as Unamuno, Langston Hughes, H.R. Hays, I. Pereda Valdés, and Pablo Neruda are of this mind as well.

274.   ———. "Nicolás Guillén. Poeta-profeta de la Revolución cubana." *Bohemia*, no. 30 (July 16, 1961), 20-21, 102, 127; (July 23, 1961), 40-43, 87-89.

In this two-part article Augier analyzes Guillén's anti-imperialist concerns as well as the poet's protest against racial discrimination. Affirms that the "black note" in Guillén's verse appears after *Cantos para soldados y sones para turistas* only as part of his total revolutionary effort.

275.   ———. "Poesía cubana y revolucionaria de Nicolás Guillén." *Cuba internacional*, no. 34 (1972), 9-15. Translated and reprinted in *Center for Cuban Studies Newsletter*, no. 2 (1973), 1-6.

Argues that Guillén's pre-Castro poetry prefigured the Revolution and that literary critics need not get tangled up in dialectical arguments to comprehend the popularity and success of his poetry. An understanding of his racial and family background is useful in explaining his poetic work.

276.   ———. "Poesía de Cuba en Nicolás Guillén: su expresión plástica." *Unión*, 1 (1962), 61-78.

Affirms that Guillén's poetry is universal but distinctively Cuban and cannot be confused with that of any other country thematically or stylistically.

277.   ———. "Prólogo: la poesía de Nicolás Guillén." Nicolás Guillén. *Obra poética (1920-1972)* (see No. 251), pp. xii-lx.

One of Augier's most recent statements on Guillén's poetry. Includes substantial comment on some of Guillén's work published in book form for the first time as well as on some of Guillén's latest work.

278.   ———. "Prólogo." Nicolás Guillén. *Prosa de prisa* (see No. 254), pp. vii-xll.

Reviews Guillén's journalistic biography filling in background information on the prose pieces (arranged chronologically) that Guillén the poet-journalist has written over the years.

279. ————. "Raíz cubana de Nicolás Guillén." *La última hora*, no. 23 (July 10, 1952), 6. Reprinted in *Recopilación de textos sobre Nicolás Guillén*. Edited by Nancy Morejón (see No. 261), pp. 139-146.

Believes Guillén's poetry illustrates the several stages ethnic elements pass through in Cuba to arrive at the final stage of the process, namely, total integration into a single national reality.

280. ————. "The Cuban Poetry of Nicolás Guillén." Translated by Joseph Bernstein. *Phylon*, 12 (1952), 32-38.

Considers April 20, 1930, to be a decisive date in the history of Cuban literature as on that day the poems of Guillén's *Motivos de son* were first published in the Sunday edition of the *Diario de la Marina*. Traces his poetry from its folkloric beginning to the continental and universal proportions it later reached.

281. Boti, Regino. "La poesía cubana de Nicolás Guillén." *Revista bimestre cubana*, 34 (1932), 343-353.

Writes that the appearance of Guillén's rhythmic and musical *Motivos de son* revolutionized Cuban poetry and completed the ethnic representation of the total population in literature. Does not see any literary relationship between Guillén and Langston Hughes other than that they both wrote poetry.

282. Campaña, Antonio. "Nicolás Guillén, sones y angustias." *Atenea*, 85 (1946), 444-458.

Considers Guillén's poetry to be a social and human expression of mulatto Cuba, a poetry that has restored the Black to recognition in that country. Describes his poetry as combative and rhythmic and at times sexual.

283. Cartey, Wilfred. "Cómo surge Nicolás Guillén en las Antillas." *Universidad de Antioquia*, 34 (1958), 257-274.

Reviews the "new spirit" in the 1920's in West Indian art and literature that focused on the African heritage. Discusses the emergence of Nicolás Guillén and his poetry within the context of this spirit.

284.   Casas Pereyra, I. "Nicolás Guillén, mirado desde lejos."
       Nuestra raza, no. 70 (June 30, 1939), 4-5.

285.   Castilla, Belarmino. "Palabras en el homenaje a Nicolás
       Guillén." *Recopilación de textos sobre Nicolás Guillén*.
       Edited by Nancy Morejón (see No. 261), pp. 63-70.

       A speech in homage to Guillén from a representative
       of the Central Committee of the Communist party on the
       occasion of the poet's seventieth birthday. Lauds the
       revolutionary consciousness-raising impact Guillén's
       verse has had on the masses over the years.

286.   Coin, Jeanette B. "Social Aspects of Black Poetry in
       Luis Palés Matos, Nicolás Guillén and Manuel del
       Cabral." Ph.D. dissertation, New York University,
       1976. 245pp.

       Traces early and recent black poetry in the Caribbean
       (including the poetic and ideological development of
       Nicolás Guillén). Relates the development of this po-
       etry to such concerns as domestic and foreign exploita-
       tion and the fight against it and to such events from
       the 1930's to the 1960's that affected the literature
       as the rise of Blacks in Africa, the Civil Rights move-
       ment in the United States, and the changes in the poli-
       tical situation in the Caribbean.

287.   Cossío, Adolfina. "Los recursos rítmicos en la poesía
       de Nicolás Guillén." *Santiago*, no. 5 (1971), 177-
       222.

       Analyzes the ways Guillén achieves rhythmic effects
       in his poetry. Argues that few poets can match Guillén's
       feeling for rhythm, a rhythm that combines standard ac-
       centuation of classic Spanish prosody with African drum
       beats. Argues that the distinctive rhythmic qualities
       of the poet can best be seen in his short verse and
       that in *Motivos de son* trochaic rhythm and reiteration
       are the techniques most frequently used. Concludes
       that Guillén is, in short, a legitimate poet extremely
       conscious of technique.

288.   Coulthard, G.R. "Nicolás Guillén and West Indian Negri-
       tude." *Caribbean Quarterly*, 16 (1970), 52-57.

       Argues that Guillén's rejection of black or counter-
       racism sets him apart from black writing in the West Indies
       and North America; that counter-racialism is not a West

Indian phenomenon; that in all Latin American countries
with large colored populations there has been little
racial antagonism and comparatively little interest in
Africa. Contends that Guillén's identity is national,
American, Cuban, and universal.

289. Cuellar Vizcaíno, Manuel. "El Guillén que usted no
     conoce." *La gaceta de Cuba*, 8-9 (1962), 6.

     Biographical data of the poet's early years with his
     reminiscences of personal contacts with Guillén.

290. Davis, Stephanie Jo. "Development of Poetic Techniques
     in the Works of Nicolás Guillén." Ph.D. dissertation,
     Princeton University, 1976. 296pp.

     Studies the development of key Vanguardist techniques
     visible in Guillén's poetry from 1927 on. Examines
     Guillén's "black" poems--which she sees as "secondary"
     manifestations in his poetry--within the context of
     Vanguardism, and shows how his social commitment modi-
     fies his artistic technique. Argues that his technique
     relies basically on a mixture of satire and pure whimsy.

291. DeCosta Willis, Miriam. "Nicolás Guillén and his Poetry
     for Black Americans." *Black World*, 22 (1973), 12-16.

     Traces the treatment of Afro-Americans in Guillén's
     poetry from incidents in the 1930's to Angela Davis.
     Argues that for Nicolás Guillén the black American more
     than any other symbolizes the double stigma of race and
     caste.

292. Depestre, René. "Nicolás Guillén. Orfeo negro de Cuba."
     La gaceta de Cuba, no. 74 (1969), 10-11.

     Asserts that Guillén shares with negritude the search
     for a black identity. Argues that this search is con-
     ducted within a revolutionary framework common to Whites,
     Blacks, and Mulattoes in Cuba.

293. ————. "Paseo por *El gran zoo* de Nicolás Guillén."
     Por la Revolución, por la poesía. Havana: Instituto
     del Libro, 1969, pp. 167-171.

     Traces the revolutionary impulse throughout Guillén's
     poetry, particularly in *El gran zoo*, where the poet cages
     or tames the principal monsters that dehumanize our
     lives, a process Depestre considers to be the most pro-
     found task of the twentieth century.

294. Ellis, Keith. "Literary Americanism and the Recent Po-
      etry of Nicolás Guillén." *University of Toronto Quar-*
      terly, 45 (1976), 1-18.

      Discusses Spanish American literary theories and traces
      the origin of Spanish American commitment to socio-polit-
      ical questions while examining the recent work of Nico-
      lás Guillén in the light of these theories. Thinks
      Guillén's poetry disproves the view that committed liter-
      ature is lacking in artistic method. Concludes that
      Guillén's poetry is perfectly adapted to the needs of
      Cuba at a specific historical moment and as such repre-
      sents a new stage in the practice of literary American-
      ism.

295. ————. "Nicolás Guillén. Interview with Keith Ellis."
      Jamaican Journal, 7 (1973), 17-19.

      Guillén in this interview gives details of his life
      from childhood on. Admits that he read some of the
      writing of Afro-American authors early in this century
      but does not believe he was influenced by them in his
      Motivos de son and his *Sóngoro cosongo*. Does not be-
      lieve Langston Hughes influenced his work. Says that
      his "Oda a Kid Chocolate" would not make sense in Cuba
      today, as such "negritude" poems would be considered
      racist. Asserts that political orientation in his po-
      etry is just as important as poetic technique.

296. ————. "Nicolás Guillén at Seventy." *Caribbean*
      Quarterly, 19 (1973), 87-94.

      Reviews the rash of publishing activity inside and
      outside of Cuba in honor of Guillén's seventieth birth-
      day. Addresses himself to what he considers the princi-
      pal misconceptions about Guillen's poetry, namely, that
      he is primarily an exponent of Afro-Cuban poetry and
      that since Castro his writings have been dedicated solely
      to praising the Revolution.

297. Farber de Aguilar, Helene J. "Poetry from Latin Ameri-
      ca: 'The Most Inportant Harvest of the Times.'"
      Parnassus. Poetry in Review, 1 (1973), 175-186.

      Reviews, among other books, Guillén's *Man-Making Words*,
      translated by Robert Márquez and David Arthur McMurray.
      Argues that in the selections translated, Guillén
      "emerges as an intelligent radical instead of a Caribbean
      bongo player in a trance." Insists, however, that the
      translators should emphasize that Guillén is "as impla-

cably meaningful and as implacably just as he is anti-
bourgeois." Contends that the most significant feature
of Guillén's work is its political integrity and that
his artistry excels in this sphere, much more so than
Pablo Neruda's.

298. Farrell, Joseph Richard. "Nicolás Guillén: Poet in
Search of *cubanidad*." Ph.D. dissertation, University
of Southern California, 1968. 255pp.

Argues that Nicolás Guillén chose poetry as his vehicle
to express his *cubanidad*, which Farrell defines as "the
state of being Cuban in the sense of having a deep awareness of national consciousness." Analyzes what he sees
as the main themes in Guillén's search for *cubanidad*:
(1) the mulatto heritage of the country and (2) the in-
terference of the United States.

299. Fernández Retamar, Roberto. "El son de vuelo popular."
La gaceta de Cuba, no. 9 (1962), 12-15. Reprinted in
Roberto Fernández Retamar. *El son de vuelo popular*
(see No. 259), pp. 43-78; and in *Recopilación de textos
sobre Nicolás Guillén*. Edited by Nancy Morejón (see
No. 261), pp. 177-198.

Believes Guillén has earned the title "National Poet";
that he moved to the forefront of *negrismo* to stay with
his *Motivos de son*; and that his poetry is really social
poetry that deals with racial integration, decoloniza-
tion, and revolution.

300. Ferrand, Manuel. "Raíz español de la poesía de Nicolás
Guillén." *Estudios americanos*, 8 (1954), 461-467.

Argues that since Guillén is a Mulatto his verse can
be either white or black and still be sincere. It is
this duality, he contends, that helps Guillén express
in his verse that which is authentically Spanish as
well as that which is black or Afro-Cuban.

301. Figueira, Gastón. "Dos poetas iberoamericanos de nuestro tiempo: Nicolás Guillén y Manuel del Cabral."
Revista iberoamericana, 10 (1945), 107-117.

Argues that it is the social aspect of Guillén's poetry that gives it value and human interest.

302. Florit, Eugenio. "Presencia de Cuba: Nicolás Guillén,
poeta entero." *Revista de América*, 13 (1948), 234-
248.

Underscores the seriousness of Guillén's poetry, especially beginning with *Sóngoro cosongo*, reflected
particularly in "Llegada," the symbolically entitled
poem that opens the collection.

303. Font, María Teresa. "Tres manifestaciones de especial-
      ismo poético: Federico García Lorca, Nicolás Guillén,
      y Jorge Luis Borges." *Revista iberoamericana*, 36
      (1970), 601-612.

      Examines poetry on the guitar from three different
      perspectives. Includes the sensual treatment Guillén
      gives it in "Guitarra" where the instrument appears as
      a "passionate" woman.

304. García Barrios, Constance Sparrow de. "The Image of the
      Black Man in the Poetry of Nicolás Guillén." *Blacks
      in Hispanic Literature: Critical Essays*. Edited by
      Miriam DeCosta (see No. 35), pp. 105-113.

      Considers Nicolás Guillén the only major practitioner
      of *negrista* poetry who continues to deal with the black
      man in his poetry beyond the vogue of the first third
      of this century. Contends further that Guillén created
      fictional black figures new to Spanish American litera-
      ture as well as including in his poetry such nonfictional
      Blacks as Angela Davis and Martin Luther King.

305. García Veitía, Margarita. "El nuevo bestiario." *Reco-
      pilación de textos sobre Nicolás Guillén*. Edited by
      Nancy Morejón (see No. 261), pp. 311-318.

      Sees *El gran zoo* as a logical outgrowth of Guillén's
      earlier work. Illustrates with stylistic examples ante-
      cedents that led up to this new *animalia*.

306. González-Pérez, Armando. "El sentimiento de la negritud
      en la poesía de Nicolás Guillén." *Caribe*, 2 (1977),
      47-58.

      Sees a big gap between the folkloric nature of the
      negrista poets and Guillén's socio-political emphasis,
      which is reinforced by his black view of the world.

307. ———. "Raza y eros en la poesía afrocubana de Nicolás
      Guillén." *Homenaje a Lydia Cabrera*. Edited by
      Reinaldo Sánchez (see No. 70), pp. 149-164.

      Argues that the objective of Guillén's poetry is to
      instill pride in the black man whom he approaches from
      within. To that end Guillén combats race prejudice and

describes black beauty symbolized in the black woman who
is depicted realistically through healthy, natural, and
erotic metaphors. Concludes that Guillén is far more
than a poet of black folklore, and agrees that he antedates negritude proper.

308. Hays, H.R. "Guillén y la poesía afrocubana." *Hoy*
(January 2, 1944), 1. Reprinted in *La última hora*,
no. 23 (July 10, 1952), 8-9; and in *Recopilación de
textos sobre Nicolás Guillén*. Edited by Nancy Morejón
(see No. 261), pp. 91-99.

Argues that Guillén's importance lies in the poetic
representation he gives to the mixed black-white component of Cuban society. Believes that Guillén does
not wish to be classified as a black writer only.

309. Hernández Novas, Raúl. "La más reciente poesía de Nicolás Guillén." *Casa de las Américas*, 8 (1972), 159-
162.

Sees many of the same formal characteristics in
Guillén's poetry after the Revolution as before, including the elegy, humor, satire, irony, and the *son*
itself, which he later alternates with longer verse
forms. Focuses on *La rueda dentada* and *El diario que
a diario*.

310. Iñiquez Madrigal, Luis. "Introducción a la poesía de
Nicolás Guillén." *Antología clave de Nicolás Guillén*
(see No. 246), pp. 5-22. Reprinted and enlarged in
Nicolás Guillén. *Summa poética* (see No. 253), pp.
13-48.

Examines three aspects of Guillén's poetic creation,
namely, language, style, and themes, to determine
whether Guillén is, in fact, a "black poet." Concludes
that he is not.

311. ———. "Introducción." Nicolás Guillén. *Summa poética*
(see No. 253), pp. 13-48.

Continues to argue in this enlarged version of No.
310 that Guillén is not a black poet in language (not a
black but a Cuban language), style (*jitanjáforas* are
not just black poetic devices), and theme (more themes
other than social or racial). Contends further that
Guillén is universal because he deals with such themes
as death.

312. ———. "Las elegías de Nicolás Guillén: Elegía a
      Emmett Till." *Cuadernos de filología*, no. 1 (1968),
      47-58.

      Chooses the *Elegía a Emmett Till* to illustrate how
      Guillén achieves artistry without resorting to the
      folkloric aspects that traditional criticism accepts as
      characteristic of his verse.

313. ———. "Poesía última de Nicolás Guillén." *Revista
      del pacífico*, 1 (1964), 73-82.

      Points out how recent criticism of Guillén's work
      dismisses his later poetry as too politically tinted
      without realizing that the social aspect has been one
      of his thematic constants throughout his career. Illus-
      trates Guillén's "tremendous artistic responsibility"
      in his later poetry. Concludes that social concern
      does not mean lack of quality.

314. Irish, J.A. George. "Notes on a Historic Visit: Nicolás
      Guillén in Jamaica." *Caribbean Quarterly*, 21 (1975),
      74-84.

      Reaffirms that Guillén, unlike other poets, especially
      white poets, did not play literary games with Afro-Cuban
      poetry but wrote from within the black experience. Re-
      views Guillén's association with Jamaica and the Uni-
      versity of the West Indies. Closes with a statement by
      the poet and includes impressions of Guillén's official
      and unofficial activities while in the country.

315. ———. "The Revolutionary Focus of Nicolás Guillén's
      Journalism." *Caribbean Quarterly*, 22 (1976), 68-77.

      Writes that Guillén always responds to universal human
      anguish and struggle. Argues that Guillén tries to
      raise or awaken revolutionary consciousness, which the
      poet considers the major issue with which the writer
      and intellectual must come to terms. It is Guillén's
      personal commitment to struggle that accounts for the
      militant spirit that permeates his prose, his speeches,
      and his poetry.

316. ———. "Nicolás Guillén's Position on Race: A Reap-
      praisal." *Revista/Review Interamericana*, 6 (Fall
      1976), 335-347.

      Analyzes Guillén the journalist as well as Guillén
      the poet. Concludes that the former pursuit throws
      light on the latter, particularly insofar as his posi-

tion on race is concerned. Argues that in his early
work Guillén wrote first and foremost as a black man
with strong racial awareness and that some of his prose
pieces form the basis for his subsequent poetic models
of racial synthesis, namely, the spiritual model, the
mulatto model, and the revolutionary model.

317. Jiménez Grullón, Juan Isidro. "Nicolás Guillén." *Seis
poetas cubanos (Ensayos apologéticos)*. Havana: Editorial Cromos, 1954, pp. 87-108.

Argues that there can be no doubt about the social
base of Guillén's poems. Affirms that the poet has the
gift of converting the most prosaic object into a poetic
subject and the poor Black into a central theme in his
literature. Concludes that Guillén is a poet who combines the folkloric and the popular with the cultured
and the erudite, that Guillén's *Elegía a Jesús Menéndez*
is a perfect poem, and that Guillén's poetry represents
the music, color, passion, happiness, anguish, and hope
of Cuba.

318. Johnson, Harvey L. "Nicolás Guillén's Portraits of
Blacks in Cuban Society." *Homage to Irving A. Leonard.
Essays on Hispanic Art, History and Literature*. Edited
by Raquel Chang-Rodríguez and Donald Yates. East
Lansing: Latin American Studies Center, Michigan
State University, 1977, pp. 197-207.

After reviewing the history of the Black in the New
World, to which, according to Johnson, the Black brought
among other things his "childlike enthusiasm," Johnson
reviews some of the pro-black poetry of Nicolás Guillén.
Recognizes that the poet has been a spokesman for the
dispossessed masses for many years. Johnson, however,
misinterprets some of Guillén's poems.

319. King, Lloyd. "Nicolás Guillén and Afrocubanism." *A
Celebration of Black and African Writing*. Edited by
Bruce King and Kolawole Ogung-besan. Zaria and Ibadan,
Nigeria: Ahmadu Bello University Press and Oxford
University Press, 1975, pp. 30-45.

Sees Guillén's *Cantos para soldados y sones para
turistas* as his most popular collection of poems in
Cuba itself, and his verse in general as prophetic of
some of the main objectives of the Cuban Revolution.
Considers Guillén's insistence on the mulatto nature of
Cuban culture to be his main contribution to the dialogue

about Cuban identity, although even some sympathetic
white Cuban writers were not persuaded by his claim
that Cuba was mulatto.

320. Knight, Franklin W. "Poet of the People." *Review*, 73
      (1973), 67-69.

321. Lazo, Raimundo. "Con motivo de una biografía de Nicolás
      Guillén." *Universidad de la Habana*, 28 (1964), 7-21.

      Considers Augier's work to be the fundamental biography
      of Guillén, but adds some of his own personal reminis-
      cences and contacts with the poet. Lazo even includes
      his memories of Guillén's father, who was also well
      known around his household.

322. López del Amo, Rolando. "Un homenaje (Notas sobre la
      temática de la poesía de Nicolás Guillén)." *Universi-
      dad de la Habana*, 196-97 (1972), 320-336.

      Summarizes themes in the poetry of Nicolás Guillén
      from *Motivos de son* to *El diario que a diario*. He con-
      siders Guillén to be one of the greatest exponents both
      artistically and politically of Cuba's revolutionary
      cause. Concludes that man--working-class man--is a basic
      theme of Guillén's poetry.

323. Lowery, D.M. "Selected Poems of Nicolás Guillén and
      Langston Hughes: Their Use of Afro-Western Folk Music
      Genres." Ph.D. dissertation, Ohio State University,
      1975. 273pp.

      Focuses on selected poems from *Motivos de son*, *Sóngoro
      cosongo*, and *West Indies Ltd.*, which are examined in
      light of their illustration of various African-derived
      musical elements. Applies concepts and techniques used
      by folklorists "who conceive of folklore as a three-di-
      mensional entity--that is, as texture, text and context."

324. Manyarrez, Froylán. "Cuba en la poesía de Nicolás
      Guillén." *Bohemia*, no. 6 (February 8, 1963), 7-9,
      106.

      Sees a powerful protest against the United States in
      Guillén's poetry, in which Cuba appears depicted in all
      its suffering. Expects Guillén's poetry one day to
      apply to the whole of Latin America in its song of
      praise of the Cuban Revolution.

325. Marinello, Juan. "Poesía negra, apuntes desde Guillén
      y Ballagas." *Poética. Ensayos en entusiasmo.*
      Madrid: Espasa Calpe, 1933, pp. 99-143.

      Contends that when Guillén writes great poetry, as in
      the poem "Llegada," he does it in a nonblack manner,
      that is, black triumph is expressed but in traditional
      Spanish verse form. Argues that in the future Guillén's
      verse will pass through a mulatto stage to a poetry or
      an art without color, Cuban color.

326. ———. "Hazaña y triunfo americanos de Nicolás
      Guillén." *Literatura hispanoamericana: hombres, medi-
      taciones.* México: Universidad Nacional de México,
      1937, pp. 79-90. Reprinted in *Recopilación de textos
      sobre Nicolás Guillén.* Edited by Nancy Morejón (see
      No. 261), pp. 283-291.

      Focuses on *Cantos para soldados y sones para turistas*,
      which he calls a new kind of revolutionary poetry that
      in the interest of all men takes on a continental and
      universal dimension.

327. Márquez, Robert. "Introducción a Guillén." *Casa de las
      Américas*, 11 (1971), 136-142. Reprinted in *Recopila-
      ción de textos sobre Nicolás Guillén.* Edited by Nancy
      Morejón (see No. 261), pp. 127-138. Also published in
      English as "Introduction" to *¡Patria o muerte!: The
      Great Zoo and Other Poems by Nicolás Guillén.* Trans-
      lated by Robert Márquez (see No. 250), pp. 13-29.

      Does not consider Guillén to be, strictly speaking, a
      poet of negritude since he, unlike Aimé Césaire and the
      poets of the French and English Caribbean, does not
      directly repudiate European cultural traditions.

328. Martí-Fuentes, Adolfo. "España en cinco esperanzas.
      Comentario a un poema de Nicolás Guillén." *Biblioteca
      José Martí*, no. 7 (1972), 55-63.

      Contends that with *España. Poema en cuatro angustias
      y una esperanza*, Nicolás Guillén raises his social po-
      etry to a universal level. Here the poet channels his
      "essential humanism" into a denunciation of fascism in
      Spain, and the book takes on--in its grand design--the
      thematic and formal structure of a Mexican mural.

329. Martínez Estrada, Ezequiel. "La poesía afrocubana de
      Nicolás Guillén." *Recopilación de textos sobre Nico-
      lás Guillén.* Edited by Nancy Morejón (see No. 261),
      pp. 71-80.

Excerpt from his book of the same name, specifically the chapter "Nosotros, vosotros y ellos." In this excerpt Martínez Estrada affirms that Guillén the mulatto poet is more Indian than African, a statement challenged by Morejón in her introduction to *Recopilación*.

330. Matheus, John F. "Langston Hughes as Translator." *College Language Association Journal*, 11 (1967), 319-330. Reprinted in *Langston Hughes, Black Genius*. Edited by Therman B. O'Daniel. New York: William Morrow, 1971, pp. 157-170.

Reviews, among others, the translations Hughes made of some representative poems from Nicolás Guillén's early works: *Motivos de son*, *Sóngoro cosongo*, and *Cantos para soldados y sones para turistas*.

331. McMurray, David Arthur. "Dos negros en el Nuevo Mundo: notas sobre el americanismo de Langston Hughes y la cubanía de Nicolás Guillén." *Casa de las Américas*, 14 (1974). 122-128.

Examines poetic visions of the two poets, and notes that each is concerned in his own way with the black experience in the New World.

332. Medina, Ciro. "Nicolás Guillén, el poeta de los negros." *Elite* (May 19, 1972). Reprinted in *De la prensa internacional* (Havana), no. 24 (June 26, 1972), 2-5.

333. Megenney, William. "Las cualidades afrocubanas en la poesía de Nicolás Guillén." *La torre*, 18 (1970), 127-138.

Believes black rhythms assimilated into the poetic tradition of Cuba form the stylistic basis for Guillén's poetry. Sees these black rhythms even in Guillén's prose.

334. Melon, Alfred. "Guillén, poeta de las síntesis." *Unión*, 9 (1970), 96-133. Reprinted in Alfred Melon. *Realidad, poesía e ideología*. Havana: Cuadernos de la Revista Unión, pp. 25-61; and in *Recopilación de textos sobre Nicolás Guillén*. Edited by Nancy Morejón (see No. 261), pp. 199-242.

Argues that Guillén is the poet of the complete Cuba, which he expresses through his poetry of synthesis. Contends that Guillén's unifying vision gives his work not just a Cuban dimension but a Caribbean, American,

and universal one as well. The Mulatto in his poetry,
he argues, is the symbol of this synthesis. Believes
this tendency toward synthesis or integration goes
back to Guillén's early Modernist verse. Singles out
expressions to illustrate this argument.

335. Michalski, André. "La 'Balada del güije' de Nicolás
Guillén: un poema garcilorquiano y magicorrealista."
Cuadernos hispanoamericanos, 274 (1973), 159-167.

Argues that Guillén's poetry is atavistic and inti-
mately linked to the primitive myths of the people.
Despite being a cultured poet Guillén becomes a shaman
whose rhythmic verses, inspired by voodoo, recite magic
formula, even in "Balada del güije," a poem written
very much in the Spanish metric tradition.

336. Morejón, Nancy, et al. "Conversación con Nicolás
Guillén." *Casa de las Américas*, 12 (1972), 123-136.
Reprinted in *Recopilación de textos sobre Nicolás
Guillén*. Edited by Nancy Morejón (see No. 261), pp.
31-61.

A collage of interviews previously given by Guillén,
including a more recent one conducted specifically for the
Recopilación. Includes Guillén's assertion that he is
not a poet of negritude. Also gives his reaction to
negative reception *Motivos de son* first received.

337. Mullen, Edward. "Langston Hughes y Nicolás Guillén: un
documento y un comentario." *Caribe*, 1 (1976), 39-48.

As a lead-in to his reprinting of Guillén's "Conversación con Langston Hughes," Mullen traces Hughes'
visits to Cuba, his reception there, and the literary
criticism dealing with the American poet's connection
with Nicolás Guillén.

338. ———. "Nicolás Guillén and Carlos Pellicer. A Case
of Literary Parallels." *Latin American Literary Review*, 3 (1975), 77-87.

Compares the highly personal vision each poet has of
his national reality. Affirms that each poet has evolved
toward a more universalized treatment of indigenous
themes and motifs. Groups the two in a generation of
poets that shares a common mythic vision of Latin America. Establishes clear-cut and immediate affinities between Pellicer and Guillén, particularly their common
declaration of opposition to racial and social injustice.

339. ———. "The Literary Reputation of Langston Hughes
in the Hispanic World." *Comparative Literature Studies*, 13 (1976), 254-269. Enlarged and reprinted as
the introduction to his *Langston Hughes in the Hispanic World*. Hamden: Archon Books, 1977, pp. 15-46.

Traces Hughes' reputation and contacts in Mexico,
Cuba, and Spain, especially the "long and fruitful"
friendship he established with Nicolás Guillén, who in-
terviewed him in Cuba, traveled with him during the
Spanish Civil War, and helped introduce him to the
Latin American public.

340. Navarro Luna, Manuel. "Un líder de la poesía revolucionaria." *Recopilación de textos sobre Nicolás
Guillén*. Edited by Nancy Morejón (see No. 261), pp.
101-115.

Argues that Guillén's *Motivos de son* was composed at
a time of growing mass awareness of racial discrimination and Yankee imperialism. Even without mentioning
the word, Guillén's poetry at that time was revolutionary because it reflected those feelings of the people.

341. Navas-Ruiz, Ricardo. "Neruda y Guillén: un caso de
relaciones literarias." *Revista iberoamericana*, 31
(1965), 251-262.

Explores literary contacts between Brazil and Spanish
America using as examples poems on Brazil by Pablo
Neruda and Nicolás Guillén. Concludes that Neruda's
"Oda a Río de Janeiro," for example, is more artisti-
cally achieved than Guillén's "Canción carioca."

342. Noble, Enrique. "Nicolás Guillén y Langston Hughes."
Nueva revista cubana. Havana: Editora del Consejo
Nacional de Cultura, 1962, pp. 3-47.

Studies comparatively and chronologically the poetic
works of the two poets. Believes biographical, ethnic,
cultural, and historical circumstances account for the
differences in the work and thought of the two authors.
Sees these differences reflected even in the titles of
some of their works.

343. Oliveira, Otto. "La mujer de color en la poesía de
Nicolás Guillén." *Homenaje a Lydia Cabrera*. Edited
by Reinaldo Sánchez (see. No. 70), pp. 165-174.

Says that black poetry is like *poesía gauchesca* in
that it is a masculine creation seen from a masculine
perspective, but unlike gauchesque poetry, black poetry
is one-sided because of its heavy emphasis on sex in its
treatment of women. Argues that the work of Nicolás
Guillén is no exception to this general rule as he, from
the beginning, looked at the black woman from a bourgeois viewpoint, focusing on external, picturesque, and
humorous aspects without reflecting any social concern
or identification with her economic or emotional plight.
Concludes that Guillén does not treat the black woman
with tenderness or lyric intimacy but, on the contrary,
reserves these qualities for women who are not black.

344.   Ortiz, Fernando. "Glosas a *Motivos de son* por Nicolás
       Guillén." *Archivos del folklore cubano*, 5 (1930),
       222-238.

       Emphasizes the folkloric nature of the *Motivos de son*.
       Argues that they are popular poems which Guillén raises
       to the level of art but which are destined because of
       their authenticity to return to the people who inspired
       them. Concludes that the *son* is different from the
       blues.

345.   Ortiz Oderigo, Nestor. "Nicolás Guillén, poeta social."
       Saber vivir, 7 (1947), 38-39. Reprinted in *Nuestra
       raza*, no. 162 (1947), 5-7.

       Recognizes that Guillén is a cultured poet but one
       who does not restrict his concern to the elite. Like
       Langston Hughes, Guillén has committed himself to the
       Black and to the worker but, unlike Hughes, Guillén
       interprets the aspirations of Blacks and Whites alike,
       whose fusion or *mulatez*, he concludes, represents the
       national mentality in Cuba.

346.   Peralta, Jaime. "España en tres poetas hispanoameri-
       canos: Neruda, Guillén, y Vallejo." *Atenea*, 45 (1968),
       37-49.

       Believes these three poets make up the ethnic composi-
       tion of Spanish America and as such represent a total
       Hispanic reaction to the Spanish Civil War.

347.   Pereda Valdés, Ildefonso. "Nicolás Guillén y el ritmo
       del *son*." *Línea de color: ensayos afroamericanos*.
       Santiago de Chile: Ercilla, 1938, pp. 143-151.

Accepts that Guillén's verse captures the rhythm and folklore of the Black but does not see much protest spirit beyond "Caña" and a few other poems. Believes Langston Hughes has set the example black writers should follow.

348. Pontrelli, Mary Castan de. "The Criollo Poetry of Nicolás Guillén." Ph.D. dissertation, Yale University, 1959. 409pp.

Argues that Guillén's poetry represents the first manifestation of a literary *criollo* poetry in Cuba. Says that Guillén's poetry is erroneously designated as Negro poetry in that his five main collections "constitute an oeuvre which is dedicated essentially to the transmutation of the Cuban idiom into a literary language which attains a universally Hispanic validity.

349. Portal, Magda. "Nicolás Guillén, poeta de Cuba. En sus setenta años." *Cuadernos americanos*, 197 (1974), 234-244.

Argues that the *mestizo* poetry of Nicolás Guillén symbolizes Cuba and that his zeal for freedom and independence is, as well, a genuine affirmation of the Latin American personality. Considers Nicolás Guillén to be all of this because he is first and foremost a poet of the people, a cultured poet, but one who places himself on the side of the proletariat racially, socially, and politically, in an anti-imperialistic stance.

350. Portuondo, José Antonio. "Canta a la revolución con toda la voz que tiene." "Prólogo." Nicolás Guillén. *Tengo* (see No. 244), pp. 7-17. Reprinted in *Crítica de la época y otros ensayos*. Havana: Universidad Central de Las Villas, 1965, pp. 188-196; and in *Recopilación de textos sobre Nicolás Guillén*. Edited by Nancy Morejón (see No. 261), pp. 303-309. Translated into English by Richard Carr in Nicolás Guillén. *Tengo* (see No. 252), pp. 7-17.

Says a revolutionary spirit has always been present in Guillén's poetry. Argues that this spirit culminates in *Tengo* and is even accentuated here in that the poet sings of the "victory over imperialism and its lackeys" while raising the artistic consciousness of the people. Contends that Guillén accomplishes this feat through an intelligent fusion of form and content.

351. ————. "Sentido elegíaco de la poesía de Guillén." *La gaceta de Cuba*. *Edición especial*. *Homenaje a Nicolás Guillén*, 8-9 (1962), 2-3.

Argues that the elegiac note which can be traced throughout Guillén's poetry is a constant in the poet's work from his post-Modernist days on, but has been obscured or overshadowed by sensuality, musicality, and other better-known aspects of his production. Contends that this elegiac note reaches its culmination in *Elegía a Jesús Menéndez*.

352. Rabanales, Ambrosio. "Relaciones asociativas en torno al 'Canto negro' de Nicolás Guillén." *Studia hispánica en honorem. Rafael Lapesa*. Edited by Eugenio Bustos et al. Madrid: Gredos, 1972. Vol. II, pp. 469-491.

Analyzes the aesthetic effect of "Canto negro." Considers the words *canto*, *negro*, and *congo*—because of the concepts and images they evoke—to be the key elements in the poem. The concepts and images evoked include music and dance, witchcraft and slavery, Africa and rhythm.

353. Rabassa, Gregory. "The Gospel of Marx According to Omolú and According to Jesus." *Parnassus. Poetry in Review*, 4 (1976), 122-129.

One of the books reviewed in this article is Guillén's *Tengo*, translated by Richard J. Carr. Argues that some of the poems in this volume have "a great deal of the 'occasional' ring to them." Believes that the poet, "like an old soldier," is at his best "when he turns to the combative tone and inveighs against the United States." In what he calls a superficial comparison Rabassa suggests that if some of Guillén's earlier work is closer to Vallejo, much of *Tengo* to a certain extent is more like Neruda.

354. Rodríguez, Nilo. "Guillén va con la música." *Recopilación de textos sobre Nicolás Guillén*. Edited by Nancy Morejón (see No. 261), pp. 171-175.

Lists several of the poems of Nicolás Guillén that have been set to music, including some of his own arrangements of Guillén's poetry.

355. Ruffinelli, Jorge. "Nuevos aportes a la poesía de Nicolás Guillén." *Revista iberoamericana de literatura*, segunda época (Montevideo), 1 (1966), 95-103.

Argues that the term "black poetry" is too tied to
race and color and as such contributes to what he sees
as a lack of understanding of what black poetry really
is within the larger framework of Hispanic American
poetry.

356. Ruscalleda Bercedoniz, Jorge María. "Recuento poético
      de Nicolás Guillén." *Sin nombre*, 4 (1976), 33-56.

      Studies briefly Guillén's poetic trajectory including
      his pre-*Motivos de son* verse and other works by the poet
      not yet well known, such as *El soldado Miguel Paz y el
      sargento José Inés*.

357. Saenz, Gerardo. "Nicolás Guillén, Langston Hughes y
      Luis Palés Matos." *Homenaje a Lydia Cabrera*. Edited
      by Reinaldo Sánchez (see No. 70), pp. 183-188.

      Concludes that Guillén sees himself as a Black, a
      Mulatto, and a Cuban while Hughes writes not as an
      American but as a Black in the United States. Palés
      Matos, he says, feels the Black and Africa in his spirit.

358. Sánchez-Rojas, Arturo. "Papá Montero: del son original
      al poema de Nicolás Guillén." *Caribe*, 1 (1976), 49-
      56.

      Examines the original song on which Guillén's poem is
      based to determine what changes the poet introduced.

359. Smart, Ian. "*Mulatez* and the Image of the Black *mujer
      nueva* in Guillén's Poetry." *Kentucky Romance Quarter-
      ly*. In press.

360. ————. "Nicolás Guillén's *Son* Poem: An African Con-
      tribution to Contemporary Caribbean Poetics." *College
      Language Association Journal*. In press.

361. ————. "The Creative Dialogue in the Poetry of Nicolás
      Guillén: Europe and Africa." Ph.D. dissertation,
      University of California, Los Angeles, 1975. 265pp.

      Reflects on the concept of *mulatez*. Sees as one of
      the larger consequences of Guillén's *mulatez* a "West
      Indianness" expressed in the poet's treatment of such
      themes as identity, race, and protest, in his use of
      humor and irony--which he believes is influenced by the
      poet's African heritage--and in his attitude toward
      love, life, and death. Considers "Mujer nueva" to be
      Guillén's most perfect example of love poetry as tribute
      to black womanhood.

362. Tamayo Vargas, Augusto. "Tres poetas de América: César Vallejo, Pablo Neruda y Nicolás Guillén." *Mercurio peruano*, 39 (1958), 483-503.

Sees these three poets as representative of America: Vallejo, with his metaphysical anguish; Neruda, with his sensuality and aggressiveness; and Nicolás Guillén, with his folklore, social poetry, and the strong rhythmic beat of the Caribbean.

363. Valdés Vivo, Raúl. "Guillén, periodista." *La gaceta de Cuba*, 89 (1963), 7.

Reveals that Nicolás Guillén is extremely meticulous in his journalistic writing. Explores various reasons why Guillén is fond of journalism.

364. Vitier, Cintio. "Breve examen de la poesía 'social' y 'negra.' La obra de Nicolás Guillén. Hallazgo del son." *Lo cubano en la poesía*. Havana: U. Central de Las Villas, 1958. 2nd ed. Havana: Instituto del Libro Cubano, 1970, pp. 412-434. Partially reprinted as "Hallazgo del son." *Recopilación de textos sobre Nicolás Guillén*. Edited by Nancy Morejón (see No. 261), pp. 147-158.

Makes his well-known statement that a typical Cuban Black resembles more a Cuban White than an African Black. Asserts further that Whites, Blacks, and Mulattoes in Cuba meet on a nonracial plane and that it is on this plane that the poetry of Nicolás Guillén operates.

365. White, Florence Estella. "*Poesía negra* in the Works of Jorge de Lima, Nicolás Guillén, and Jacques Roumain, 1927-1947." Ph.D. dissertation, University of Wisconsin, 1952.

One of the early dissertations in English on Guillén's life and work. Sets the tone for many of the comparative studies on black poetry in the Americas that followed. Precedes Augier's work but draws on correspondence with the Cuban biographer of Nicolás Guillén. Includes some critical appraisal of Guillén's prose.

366. Williams, Lorna. "The African Presence in the Poetry of Nicolás Guillén." *Africa and the Caribbean: Legacies of a Link*. Edited by Margaret E. Crahan and Franklin W. Knight. Forthcoming.

Analyzes several poems of Nicolás Guillén to illustrate his grounding in African lyric expression and his adherence to popular images and attitudes toward Africa that were prevailing in the Caribbean at the time he wrote his early work. Reviews Guillén's later success in capturing the African continent in a variety of attitudes seen from the perspective of a "Yoruba from Cuba."

See also Nos. 12, 26, 29-32, 37, 41, 43, 47, 50, 51, 53, 55, 60, 62, 64, 65, 71, 80, 81, 83, 86-88, 93, 95, 97, 99, 100, 102, 103, 105-109, 112, 114, 115, 117, 122, 124, 126, 129, 130, 132, 133, 135, 142, 144, 147, 148, 150-153, 155-157, 159-161, 163, 164, 166, 172, 173, 175, 179-181, 186, 188, 189.

HERNANDEZ, GASPAR OCTAVIO   (Panama, 1893-1918)

A. Works

367.   *Melodías del pasado*. Panama: Esto y Aquello, 1915.
       94pp.

368.   *Iconografía*. Panama: Esto y Aquello, 1916. 145pp.

369.   *Cristo y la mujer de Sichar*. Panama: Esto y Aquello,
       1916. 32pp.

370.   *La copa de amatista*. Panama: Imprenta Nacional, 1923.
       Published posthumously. 99pp.

371.   *Poesías escogidas*. Edited by Octavio Augusto Hernández.
       Panama: Imprenta Nacional, 1955. 36pp.

372.   *Obras selectas*. Edited by Octavio Augusto Hernández.
       Panama: Imprenta Nacional, 1966. 589pp.

B. Criticism

1. Bibliography

373.   Hernández, Octavio Augusto. "Bibliografía de Gaspar
       Octavio Hernández." Gaspar Octavio Hernández. *Obras
       selectas* (see No. 372), pp. 539-578.

       Despite the title, this bibliography includes an extensive list of works not just by but about the poet as well. It is designed to complement the *Obras selectas* but is, by itself, an important research tool. Contains original dates of publication for individual items of prose and poetry.

2. Books

374. Bolaños Guevara, Mercedes Gabriela. *Dos poetas panameños: Ricardo Miró y Gaspar Octavio Hernández.* Panama: Imprenta Nacional,' 1970. 253pp.

A thematic and stylistic analysis of Hernández's poetry. Argues that his fame should not rest on his patriotic verse alone. Judges his poetry, despite some exceptions, to be of remarkably high quality considering his limited educational background. Notes Hernández's preference for the color white as a symbol of purity.

375. Peña, Concha. *Gaspar Octavio Hernández. "Poeta del Pueblo."* Panama: Imprenta Nacional, 1953. 245pp.

A biographical study but one that pays some attention to the work of the poet, whose preferred poetic form, Peña writes, was the sonnet. Believes Hernández identified with heroic Blacks from the past despite his cult of whiteness. Considers the bust of him raised in the city of Panama a fitting honor rendered to a poet whose extreme patriotism explains why he has been called "Poet of the People."

3. Articles, Shorter Studies, and Dissertations

376. Alvarado de Ricord, Elsie. "El sentimiento patriótico en la poesía panameña." *Lotería*, no. 72 (1961), 39-44.

Disagrees with the negative assessment made of Gaspar Octavio Hernández's poetry by Roque Javier Laurenza. Argues that Hernández's genuinely patriotic poetry is representative of the Panamanian people.

377. Augusto Gómez O., Ivan. "Estudio de la poesía de Gaspar Octavio Hernández. Acompañado de un intento de análisis estilístico de su 'Poema del pasado, del presente, y del porvenir: cristo y la mujer de Sichar.'" Thesis, University of Panama, 1956-57. 115pp.

Argues that the poet's life is expressed in his poetry and that no other biographical information is necessary. Says that Hernández continues the tradition of El Mulato Urriola, Simón Rivas, and Federico Escobar while representing at the same time the best of Modernist verse in Panama. His Modernism, however, unlike that of others, is deeply rooted in nationalist themes.

378. Blásquez de Pedro, J.M. "A la memoria de Gaspar Octavio
      Hernández." *Diario de Panamá* (November 13, 1920).
      Reprinted in Gaspar Octavio Hernández. *Obras selectas*
      (see No. 372), pp. 3-21.

      Reviews the author's life, his poetry, and his prose.
      Emphasizes that Hernández, orphaned at an early age,
      was largely self-taught and that his Modernist tenden-
      cies led him to emphasize form and to copy Rubén Darío.

379. García S., Ismael. "Gaspar Octavio Hernández." *Historia
      de la literatura panameña.* Mexico: Universidad Na-
      cional Autónoma de México, 1964, pp. 68-71.

      Sees the poet's biography as the key to his poetry in
      that the grief expressed is the accurate reflection of
      a bitter existence. Sees death as one of the poet's
      frequent themes.

380. Hernández, Octavio Augusto. "Introducción." Gaspar
      Octavio Hernández. *Obras selectas* (see No. 372), pp.
      ix-xvi.

      Admires the perseverance and will to overcome handi-
      caps that could have prevented his father from achieving
      an honored place in Panama's literary history. High-
      lights the life, works, and patriotism of one who "was
      born, suffered, and died."

381. Korsi, Demetrio. "Elegía en prosa del poeta." Gaspar
      Octavio Hernández. *La copa de amatista* (see No. 370).
      Reprinted in Gaspar Octavio Hernández. *Obras selectas*
      (see No. 372), pp. 99-108.

      Characterizes Hernández as a great black swan with a
      white soul. Korsi speaks of the "deep and legitimate"
      friendship he shared with the poet, of the bohemian
      period of their lives, and of Hernández's melancholic,
      romantic, and Modernist nature.

382. Laurenza, Roque Javier. "Gaspar Octavio Hernández o el
      deseo." *Los poetas de la generación republicana.*
      Panama: Ediciones del Grupo "Pasaje," 1933, pp. 96-
      105.

      Believes that the poet overdoes his Modernist musi-
      cality, that he felt inferior because of his color, and
      that the cult of whiteness in his poetry was an escape
      from his color, as was his whole act of writing. For
      these reasons he considers Hernández's poetry to be
      lacking in authenticity. Dismisses it as a mere pose.

383. López de Berbey, Yolanda. "Gaspar Octavio Hernández
     (Apuntes biográficos y críticos)." Thesis, Univer-
     sity of Panama, 1960. 79pp.

     Affirms that Hernández was strongly influenced by
     Rubén Darío but that the Panamanian was more romantic
     in attitude than Darío, though just as concerned about
     the "beautiful form" Modernist poetry should have. Ar-
     gues that Hernández's blackness was the source of his
     frustrations, that he did not identify with black
     people, that his greatest service was to the national-
     ist cause, and he and Rubén Darío shared similar res-
     ervations about the United States.

384. Miró, Ricardo. "Gaspar Octavio Hernández." *Teoría de
     la patria.* Buenos Aires: Talleres Gráficos de Se-
     bastián Amorrortu e Hijos, 1947, pp. 83-94.

     Recognizes the need to determine the black contribution
     to Panamanian letters. Contends that Gaspar Octavio
     Hernández, one of Panama's most popular poets, is but
     one in a long line of black poets in the country. Per-
     ceives his poetry as characterized by three fundamental
     aspects: Modernist themes and techniques, socio-politi-
     cal considerations, and patriotism. Also considers
     Hernández to be the one poet of his time to have been
     interested in the work of other Panamanian writers and
     in the problems of Panamanian literature.

385. Olivares, Eneida. "Gaspar Octavio Hernández como
     cuentista." Thesis, University of Panama, 1954.
     89pp.

     Strives to shift focus from Hernández the poet to
     Hernández the *cuentista* as she considers his prose
     stories to be of a quality equal to his poetry. In-
     cludes a selection of his prose pieces.

386. Sinán, Rogelio. "La poesía panameña." *Cuadernos ameri-
     canos,* 120 (1962), 52-67.

     Argues that Hernández's cult of whiteness was more the
     result of personal frustration than a literary pose.

See also Nos. 64, 88, 138.

LLANOS ALLENDE, VICTORIO   (Peru, 1897-   )

    A. Works

387. *Marimbambe.* Barcelona: Ediciones Rumbos, 1962. 112pp.

    B. Criticism

388. Díaz de Andino, Juan. "El más grande poeta negro puer-
      torriqueño." *El mundo* (Suplemento) (December 1,
      962), 2.

      Reviews the poet's life, activities, and work. Sees
      his verse as the sensitive, humble, and noble expression
      of a religious poet, one noted for his humanism.

389. Romeu, José A. "Prólogo." *Marimbambe.* Barcelona:
      Ediciones Rumbos, 1962, pp. 5-8.

      Characterizes Llanos' poetry as uneven but popular
      with authentic Afro-Antillean rhythms and at times so-
      cial protest themes.

See also No. 54.

MANZANO, JUAN FRANCISCO   (Cuba, 1797-1854)

    A. Works

390. *Cantos a Lesbia: poesías líricas.* Havana, 1821.

391. *Flores pasajeras.* Havana, 1830.

392. *Poems by a Slave in the Island of Cuba Recently Libera-
      ted.* Translated by Richard Madden. London: Ward,
      1840. 188pp.

393. *Zafira: tragedia en cuatro actos.* Havana: Imprenta de
      Mier y Terán, 1842. 103pp.

      This work, Manzano's only play, was published in 1962
      by the Consejo Nacional de Cultura so that future gener-
      ations will have at their disposal the complete works
      of the slave poet.

394. *Autobiografía, cartas y versos.* Edited by José L.
      Franco. Havana: Municipio de la Habana, 1937. 92pp.

      Though circulated in manuscript and translated into
      English in the nineteenth century, this version of the

Autobiografía was published, complete with orthographical peculiarities, for the first time in Spanish in 1937. This work was published again in a new edition in 1972 in Cuba by the Instituto Cubano del Libro as part of Manzano's complete *Obras*. His play, *Zafira*, was also reprinted in this volume.

395. *Autobiografía de un esclavo*. Edited by Ivan A. Schulman. Madrid: Ediciones Guadarrama, S.A., 1975. 117pp.

    A modernized text for the "contemporary" reader. Based on the José L. Franco edition of the original manuscript, which was first published in 1937 (see No. 394).

B. Criticism

396. Franco, José L. "Juan Francisco Manzano, el poeta esclavo y su tiempo." *Juan Francisco Manzano. Autobiografía, cartas y versos* (see No. 394), pp. 9-32. Reprinted with slight changes in Franco's 1972 edition of Manzano's *Obras*. Havana: Instituto Cubano del Libro, pp. 199-227.

    The text of a speech delivered in 1936. Offers basic biographical and literary information on Manzano and his time. Concludes that Manzano, once freed, became disillusioned with his freedom as continued persecutions and racial discrimination enveloped the poet in a resigned melancholy that he was unable to escape.

397. Guirao, Ramón. "Poetas negros y mestizos de la época esclavista." *Bohemia* (August 26, 1934), 43-44, 123-124.

    Contends that oppressive social conditions during slavery times were more to blame for shortcomings of black poets than the poets themselves. Blacks were watched and not allowed even basic elementary education. For these reasons such slave poets as Juan Francisco Manzano, he argues, were unable to do very much to improve their lives and that of other slaves.

398. Leante, César. "Dos obras antiesclavistas cubanas." *Cuadernos americanos*, 4 (1976), 175-188.

    Points out ideological and biographical similarities between Francisco the fictional creation in Suárez y Romero's *Francisco* and Juan Francisco Manzano the real person, who stars in his own *Autobiografía*. Both books

were written at the instigation of Del Monte, which
accounts, he argues, for these similarities.

399. Matas, Julio. "La *Zafira* de Juan Francisco Manzano."
      Unión, no. 7 (1962), 96-98.

      Asserts that *Zafira*, Manzano's only dramatic piece, is
      not, on the whole, a good work, although his rudimentary
      technique does produce some good lyric passages.

400. Moliner, Israel. "Manzano: la denuncia del silencio."
      Juan Francisco Manzano. *Obras*. Edited by José L.
      Franco. Havana: Instituto Cubano del Libro, 1972,
      pp. 227-231.

      Points out the hypocrisy and timidity of Del Monte
      and his friends who denounced the horrors of slavery
      but were reluctant to accept slaves as human beings
      with the same rights as they enjoyed. To do so would
      have meant the end of benefits they themselves derived
      from the institution. Compares their attitude then
      with similar ones held later at the time of the Cuban
      Revolution, when some wanted revolution but "not too
      much." Contends that Manzano's silence after the
      Escalera purge stands as a testimony of the brutality
      of a colonial system.

401. Schulman, Ivan. "Introducción." Juan Francisco Manzano.
      Autobiografía de un esclavo (see No. 395), pp. 9-54.

      Compares Manzano in his *Autobiografía* to Esteban in
      Miguel Barnet's *Biografía de un cimarrón* (1967). Con-
      cludes that the former's psychological orientation was
      white and the latter's black. Establishes three key
      moments in Manzano's life: his birth, his freedom, and
      his writing of his *Autobiografía*. Considers the myste-
      rious disappearance of the second part of the *Autobio-
      grafía* to be as enigmatic as Manzano's relative silence
      after gaining his freedom.

See also Nos. 25, 28, 37, 42, 79, 84, 96, 100, 111, 122, 123,
128, 153, 166, 170, 173, 174, 183.

MOREJON, NANCY (Cuba, 1944-)

      A. Works

401a. *Mutaciones*. Havana: Ediciones El Puente, 1962.

401b. *Amor, ciudad atribuída*. Havana: Ediciones El Puente, 1964.

402. *Richard trajo su flauta*. Havana: Unión, 1967.

402a. *Octubre imprescindible*. Havana: Ediciones Unión, 1976.

B. Criticism

See Nos. 58, 186.

MORUA DELGADO, MARTIN   (Cuba, 1856-1910)

A. Works

403. *Sofía*. Havana: Imprenta de A. Alvarez y Compañía, 1891.
Reprint. Havana: Instituto Cubano del Libro, 1972.
194pp.

404. *La familia Unzúazu*. Havana: La Prosperidad, 1901.
325pp. Reprint. Havana: Editorial Arte y Literatura,
1975. 265pp.

405. *Obras completas*. Havana: Impresores Nosotros, 1957.
5 vols.

The first two volumes contain *Sofía* and *La familia
Unzúazu*, the two novels that were to have formed part
of a series. The other volumes contain his political
and literary essays and his translations.

B. Criticism

1. Books

406. González, Julián. *Martín Morúa Delgado. Impresiones
sobre su última novela y su gestión en la Constitu-
yente de Cuba*. Havana: Rambla y Bouza, 1902. 66pp.

One of the first studies on Morúa Delgado to concen-
trate on *La familia Unzúazu*. Contains biographical,
academic, and political commentary particularly in regard to the author's support of the Platt Amendment.

407. Horrego Estuch, Leopoldo. *Martín Morúa Delgado. Vida
y mensaje*. Havana: Comisión Nacional del Centenario
de Martín Morúa Delgado, 1959. 298pp.

Reviews the author's life and works, particularly the
political rivalry between Morúa and Juan Gualberto
Gómez. Concludes that their positions were not too far
apart. Clarifies that *Sofía* was written to correct the
negative image of Blacks that Villaverde's *Cecilia
Valdés* had left. Compares Villaverde to Morúa. The
first, he writes, merely paints a picture of what he
sees, whereas Morúa in his novels brings judgment to
bear on the slave society.

2. Articles, Shorter Studies, and Dissertations

408.   Alvarez García, Ismeldo. "Prólogo." Martín Morúa
        Delgado. *Sofía*. Havana: Instituto Cubano del Libro,
        1972, pp. vii–xii.

Argues that typical themes of the nineteenth-century
Cuban novel can be seen in Morúa Delgado's novels.
These themes, he says, are the tragedy of slavery, race
and class relations, and the at times painful integration of two different cultures. Contends further, however, that Morúa Delgado's work is different since it
is the direct testimony of a Mulatto who wrote from experience. It is this vision from within that makes his
work valuable despite its stylistic deficiencies.

409.   Baeza Flores, Alberto. "Morúa Delgado traductor."
        Obras completas de Martín Morúa Delgado (see No. 405).
        Vol. IV, pp. vii–xii.

Relates biographical circumstances (such as his stay
in the United States) in the author's life to his translations. Emphasizes especially Morúa Delgado's admiration for Toussaint L'Ouverture whose biography he translated into Spanish.

410.   ———. "*Sofía* en el escenario de la novelística de
        Cuba." *Obras completas de Martín Morúa Delgado* (see
        No. 405). Vol. I, pp. xvii–xxii.

Reviews some of the early criticism of the novel which
judges it to be generally a work of social protest that
shows novelistic promise despite a rhetorical style and
excessive melodrama.

411.   ———. "*La familia Unzúazu*: la segunda novela de
        Morúa Delgado." *Obras completas de Martín Morúa Del-
        gado* (see No. 405). Vol. II, pp. ix–xii.

Reviews some of the early criticism, which judges
this novel to be of better quality than *Sofía* stylistically and structurally.

412. ————. "Las impresiones literarias de Martín Morúa
Delgado." *Obras completas de Martín Morúa Delgado*
(see No. 405). Vol. V, pp. 7-14.

Emphasizes Morúa Delgado's social consciousness and
the importance of his essay "Las novelas del Sr. Villaverde," first published in 1892.

413. Cobb, Martha K. "An Appraisal of Latin American Slavery
Through Literature." *Journal of Negro History*, 58
(1975), 460-469.

Argues that Morúa Delgado goes beyond other abolition-
ist novelists in that his "angle of vision" is taken from
an inside position. Cobb concludes that the author
from this vantage point is better able to illustrate
"the dishonesty of a society which rationalizes slavery,
and judges and punishes its slaves by white Christian
standards which it neither practises within its own
cultural community nor in relation to its slaves and
free men of color."

414. ————. "Martín Morúa Delgado." *Negro History Bulletin*,
36 (1973), 12.

Biographical review with emphasis on Morúa Delgado's
role as a labor organizer, politician, journalist, and
novelist.

415. Deschamps Chapeaux, Pedro. "Prólogo." Martín Morúa
Delgado. *La familia Unzúazu*. Havana: Editorial Arte
y Literatura, 1975, pp. 10-17.

Argues that Morúa Delgado's *La familia Unzúazu* is a
good reflection of Cuban society between 1868 and 1878.
Believes that it represents in effect Cuban society in
microcosm, a society divided among Blacks and Whites,
slaves and free men, creoles and Spaniards. Contends
that *La familia Unzúazu* with its economic and ethnic
themes is a much more ambitious novel than *Sofía*. Sees
the author's thought amply expressed in both novels.

416. González Puente, José. "Prólogo." *Obras completas de
Martín Morúa Delgado* (see No. 405). Vol. I, pp. ix-
xiv.

Contends that Morúa Delgado's entire life was devoted
to combatting prejudice and to bringing about integration in Cuba.

417. Guillén, Nicolás. "Martín Morúa Delgado." *Bohemia*
      (Sept. 1, 1949). Reprinted in Martín Morúa Delgado.
      La familia Unzúazu. Havana: Editorial Arte y Litera-
      tura, 1975, pp. 245-265.

      In this biographical overview Guillén observes from
      the outset that Morúa Delgado was the first and last
      black Cuban to reach the high post of President of the
      Senate. Emphasizes the social meaning and historical
      focus of Morúa Delgado's work, which Guillén says are
      more important than style and plot. Reviews his journal-
      istic work, his political rivalry with Juan Gualberto
      Gómez, and other polemical aspects of his life and works.

418. Hernández-Miyares, Julio E. "El tema negro en las
      novelas naturalistas de Martín Morúa Delgado." *Homenaje
      a Lydia Cabrera*. Edited by Reinaldo Sánchez, et al.
      (see No. 70). Miami: Ediciones Universal, 1978, pp.
      211-220.

      Concentrates primarily on *Sofía*, which he says has
      some of Balzac's realism but more of Zola's radical
      naturalism. Says that Morúa Delgado took care not to
      commit the same mistakes Villaverde made in his *Cecilia
      Valdés*. Argues that while *Cecilia Valdés* stands as the
      great novel of nineteenth-century Cuban literature,
      Morúa Delgado's *Sofía* has the distinction of being the
      first naturalist novel in Cuba and the Spanish Caribbean.

419. Mesa Rodríguez, Manuel I. *Martín Morúa Delgado*. Havana:
      Imprenta "El Siglo," 1956. 51pp.

      A speech in which the author argues that Morúa Delgado
      was a learned man, a polyglot, and polemical figure
      whose presence in politics and literature throughout his
      lifetime could not be overlooked. Underscores the
      friendship between Morúa Delgado and Juan Gualberto Gómez
      that belied their public differences. Contends that
      Sofía and *La familia Unzúazu* are high quality novels
      that merit reprinting and wider circulation.

420. Portuondo, Aleuda T. *Vigencia, política y literatura
      de Martín Morúa Delgado (un ensayo sobre el gran negro
      cubano)*. Miami: Ediciones Universal, 1978. 16pp.

An essay dedicated to Lydia Cabrera, whose father,
the author adds, made possible the original publication
of Morúa Delgado's *Sofía*. Asserts that Morúa Delgado's
work is not as well known as it should be in Cuba and
abroad. Reviews the life of this man whom she considers
a Cuban of the highest integrity, in whose novel *Sofía*
one can see expressed a vision regarding problems facing
Cuban society. Does not believe Morúa Delgado was a
race-minded person since he gives negative aspects of
Whites and Blacks alike in his work. Concludes with a
consideration of Morúa Delgado and Villaverde and contends that parallels between *Cecilia Valdés* and *Sofía*
should not be attempted.

421. Rodríguez Figueroa, Iraida. *"Sofía."* *Universidad de la
Habana*, 1 (1973), 210–215.

Uses Morúa Delgado's criticism of Villaverde's
Cecilia Valdés as a point of departure for his discussion of what Morúa Delgado attempted to do in *Sofía*.
Concludes that Villaverde's vision was that of an upper-
class White and Morúa Delgado's that of an intelligent
Mulatto whose mother had been a slave. Believes that
the merit of *Sofía* is more historical than literary.

See also Nos. 7, 84, 96, 100, 123, 124, 128, 166.

OBESO, CANDELARIO (Colombia, 1849–1884)

A. Works

422. *Cantos populares de mi tierra* (1880). Bogotá: Biblioteca Popular de Cultura Colombiana, 1950. 253pp.

Also contains *Lectura para ti*, a collection of prose
and poetry, and his *Lucha de la vida*, a long autobio-
graphical poem.

B. Criticism

1. Books

423. Caraballo, Vicente. *El negro Obeso (Candelario).
Apuntes biográficos y escritos varios*. Bogotá: Editorial A.B.C., 1943. 202pp.

Undertakes this study to give Obeso the exposure due
him. Traces his life from infancy and provides information on circumstances surrounding his publications.

Reviews the literature and conflicting opinion concern-
ing the poet's death, particularly the suicide thesis.
Concludes with a brief analysis of his work asserting
that *Cantos populares de mi tierra* suffices to assure
Obeso a place in the world of letters.

2. Articles, Shorter Studies, and Dissertations

424. Añez, Julio. "Candelario Obeso." Candelario Obeso.
      Cantos populares de mi tierra (see No. 422), pp. 7-
      10.

      Emphasizes the hard times Obeso had to overcome to
      achieve the success he enjoyed. Underscores the strong
      attachment the poet felt for his mother. Does not be-
      lieve he committed suicide.

425. Guillén, Nicolás. "Sobre Candelario Obeso." *Hoy* (July
      10, 1960). Reprinted in Nicolás Guillén. *Prosa de
      prisa 1929-1972* (see No. 254). Vol. III, pp. 333-
      335.

      Sees Obeso's *cantos* and his own *sones* as part of a
      long tradition in Hispanic literature dating back to
      Góngora and to Sor Juana and before.

426. Vives Guerra, Julio y José Velázquez. "Crónicas del
      siglo XIX. De la historia del poeta negro (Candelario
      Obeso)." *Carteles* (March 10, 1943).

See also Nos. 12, 51, 52, 68, 80, 98, 125.

ORTIZ, ADALBERTO (Ecuador, 1914-)

A. Works

427. *Juyungo. Historia de un negro, una isla y otros negros.*
      Buenos Aires: Editorial Americalee, 1943. 268pp.
      Quito: Editorial Casa de la Cultura Ecuatoriana,
      1957. 317pp. Guayaquil: Editorial Casa de la Cultura
      Ecuatoriana, 1968. Barcelona: Seix Barral, 1976.
      286pp.

428. *Tierra, son y tambor: cantares negros y mulatos.* Mexico:
      La Cigarra, 1945. 81pp. Guayaquil: Casa de la Cul-
      tura Ecuatoriana, 1953. 100pp.

429. *Camino y puerto de la angustia.* Mexico: Isla, 1945.
72pp.

430. *Los contrabandistas.* Mexico: Colección Lunes, 1945.
35pp.

431. *La mala espalda. Once relatos de aquí y allá.* Guayaquil: Casa de la Cultura Ecuatoriana, 1952. 161pp.

432. *El vigilante insepulto.* Guayaquil: Casa de la Cultura
Ecuatoriana, 1954. 32pp.

433. *El animal herido. Poesía completa.* Quito: Casa de la
Cultura Ecuatoriana, 1959. 1961. Reprint. Nendeln:
Kraus, 1970.

434. *El espejo y la ventana.* Quito: Casa de la Cultura Ecuatoriana, 1967. 315pp. Guayaquil: Casa de la Cultura
Ecuatoriana, 1970. 280pp.

Ortiz's second novel.

435. *La entundada y cuentos variados.* Quito: Casa de la
Cultura Ecuatoriana, 1971. 207pp.

436. *Fórmulas, El vigilante insepulto, Tierra, son y tambor.*
Quito: Casa de la Cultura Ecuatoriana, 1973. 125pp.

B. Criticism

437. Codina, Iverna. "Adalberto Ortiz y la presencia del
negro." *América y la novela.* Buenos Aires: Ediciones
Cruz del Sur, 1964, pp. 115-117.

Characterizes *Juyungo* as a polemical and poetic novel
that exhorts the Black to assume manhood.

437a. Díaz, Oswaldo. "Relaciones sociales dentro de una
sociedad multiracial." *El negro y el indio en la
sociedad ecuatoriana.* Bogotá: Ediciones Tercer Mundo,
1978, pp. 13-33.

Bases his study on Ortiz's novel *Juyungo*. Sees in
this novel a representative cross section of Ecuadorian
society. Argues that the title of the work itself reveals much about Ecuador's multiracial society since
juyungo is a word the Cayapa Indians use to refer to
Blacks.

438. Donahue, Moraima de Semprún. "A Word with Adalberto
      Ortiz." *Américas*, 30 (1978), 49-51.

      States that the literary work of Adalberto Ortiz is
      influenced by Africa. Includes a recent interview with
      the writer, who defends *Juyungo* against such critics as
      Luis Alberto Sánchez who are of the opinion that the
      lyricism in the novel is too sustained to be enduring.

439. Gallegos Lara, J. "Raza, poesía y novela de Adalberto
      Ortiz." *Tierra, son y tambor*. Mexico: La Cigarra,
      1945, pp. 7-18. Reprinted in Adalberto Ortiz. *El
      animal herido*. Quito: Casa de la Cultura Ecuatoriana,
      1959, pp. 13-20.

      Sees in Ortiz's humanity a resemblance to Richard
      Wright. Identifies drum beat rhythms as Ortiz's origi-
      nal contribution to traditional Spanish prosody. Con-
      siders *Juyungo* to be an authentic depiction of the peo-
      ple of Esmeraldas. Concludes that Ortiz created a novel
      with literary value without resorting to Gongoristic
      prose and pseudo-intellectual techniques.

440. González Contreras, Gilberto. "La angustia escondida
      de Adalberto Ortiz." *Letras de Ecuador*, no. 11 (1946),
      8-9.

      Argues that Ortiz writes poetry out of his anguished
      experiences in his native Esmeraldas and that the real
      protagonists of *Juyungo* are the jungle, the island, the
      river, and other forces of nature.

441. Heise, Karl H. "Adalberto Ortiz." *El grupo de Guaya-
      quil. Arte y técnica de sus novelas sociales*.
      Madrid: Playor, S.A., 1975, pp. 117-122.

      Considers Ortiz a member of the Group of Guayaquil.
      Also considers him a poet in *Juyungo* because of its
      persistent lyricism. Sees Juyungo as a symbol of the
      Ecuadorian Black, but argues that Ortiz makes his poetic
      language and expression too refined to be convincing.

442. Lorenz, Gunter. "Adalberto Ortiz." *Diálogo con América
      Latina*. Valparaíso: Ediciones Universitarias de Val-
      paraíso, 1972, pp. 319-332.

      States that in *Juyungo* Ortiz introduced a new proto-
      type in Spanish American literature, one that shows
      affinity with the *indigenismo* of Miguel Angel Asturias
      and Ciro Alegría. Their works deal with economic ex-

ploitation and social discrimination. Ortiz, he argues,
writes in a style that can be called "modified magical
realism." Includes an interview with the author, who
considers himself a "humanistic writer."

443. Mainer, José-Carlos. "Prólogo." Adalberto Ortiz.
Juyungo. Barcelona: Seix Barral, 1976, pp. 7-13.

Compares Ortiz's *Juyungo* to Alejo Carpentier's *Ecué
Yamba O* and to Ramón Díaz Sánchez's *Cumboto* and concludes that Ortiz's Lastre stands out in contrast as an
epic hero. Argues that Lastre's glorious death is
clouded with ambiguity and that the novel operates on
three stylistic levels: epic, popular, and lyric, and
that the "Oído y ojo de la selva" sections that introduce each chapter are the most original and innovative
aspects of the novel.

444. Richard, Renaud. "*Juyungo* de Adalberto Ortiz, ou de la
haine raciale à la lutte contre l'injustice." *Bulletin
hispanique*, 72 (1970), 152-170.

Identifies four stages in the evolution of Juyungo:
(1) adolescence or the demystification stage, (2) a
period of racial hatred, (3) a period where racial hatred is transformed into a passion for social justice,
(4) a final stage where Juyungo's fight against injustice carries over into a nationalistic participation in
the defense of his country against a military invasion
by Peru.

445. Thiel, Vitalina Coello. "La condición del mestizo
ecuatoriano a través de la narrativa de Othon Castillo
y Adalberto Ortiz." Ph.D. dissertation, University
of Southern California, 1975. 384pp.

Considers *Juyungo* an epic document of the province of
Esmeraldas, one written in lyric prose with qualities
of sonorous musicality. Studies style and literary
technique and focuses on the treatment of the Ecuadorian
Mestizo seen as victim of social, political, and economic problems of the country. Contends that Ortiz's
second novel, *El espejo y la ventana*, illustrates the
clash and the fusion of the three races that make up
the composition of Ecuadorian society: the European,
the Indian, and the Black, but with more emphasis on
the Mulatto and the Mestizo, dominant characters in the
work.

See also Nos. 36, 65, 103, 106, 110, 121, 126, 143, 169, 173, 184.

PALACIOS, ARNOLDO (Colombia)

A. Works

446. *Las estrellas son negras.* Bogotá: Editorial Iqueima,
     1949. 190pp. 2nd ed. Bogotá: Editorial Revista
     Colombiana Ltd., 1971. 186pp.

447. *La selva y la lluvia.* Moscow: Ediciones en Lenguas
     Extranjeras, 1958. 223pp.

B. Criticism

448. Curcio Altamar, Antonio. "La novela contemporánea."
     Evolución de la novela colombiana. Bogotá: Instituto
     Caro y Cuervo, 1957, pp. 187-218.

     Considers Arnoldo Palacios' *Las estrellas son negras*
     the most completely naruralistic novel ever produced in
     Colombia, both in style and in subject matter.

449. Restrepo Millán, J.M. "Prólogo." Arnoldo Palacios.
     Las estrellas son negras. Bogotá: Editorial Revista
     Colombiana Ltd., 1971, pp. 9-22.

     Argues that Palacios draws directly on the people,
     nature, and problems of the Chocó region of Colombia
     which he expresses in his *Las estrellas son negras.*
     Palacios does this, he contends, without the kind of
     excessive intellectualizing that undermines many novels,
     particularly novels that claim to be Colombian.

See also Nos. 12, 65, 76, 90, 94, 145, 146, 162, 561.

PEDROSO, REGINO (Cuba, 1897-)

A. Works

450. *Nosotros.* Havana, 1933. 70pp.

451. *Antología poética (1918-1938).* Havana: Municipio de la
     Habana, 1939. 144pp.

452. *Más allá canta el mar.* Havana: Editorial la Verónica,
     1939. 93pp.

453. *Bolívar: sinfonía de libertad. Poema.* Havana: P. Fernández, 1945. 40pp.

454. *El ciruelo de Yan Pei Fu; poemas chinos.* Havana, 1955. 185pp.

455. *Poemas. Antología.* Havana: Ediciones Unión, 1966. 300pp.

B. Criticism

456. Ballagas, Emilio. "Notas sobre Regino Pedroso." *Revista cubana*, 31 (1957), 83-85.

    Divides Pedroso's poetry into periods, namely, an oriental, a social, and a universal phase.

457. Bueno, Salvador. "Regino Pedroso." *Bohemia*, no. 32 (August 7, 1970), 4-7.

    Recounts an interview held with the poet in which Pedroso declares himself to be predominantly Chinese because of the stronger influence from his father. In this interview Pedroso says that when he wrote of the Black in "Hermano negro" he addressed what was universally human in the subject rather than what was specifically Black.

458. Figueira, Gastón. "Pedroso." *Poetas y escritores de América.* Montevideo, 1963. Reprinted in *Bohemia*, no. 32 (August 7, 1970), 9.

    States that Pedroso has not insisted on the theme of black suffering because he said all he had to say on the subject in his poem "Hermano negro." There was no need to repeat himself on this theme since there were so many new themes to explore.

459. Guillén, Nicolás. "Prólogo." Regino Pedroso. *Poemas. Antología.* Havana: Ediciones Unión, 1966, pp. 7-8.

    Affirms that there are at least three different Pedrosos: Pedroso the post-Modernist, Pedroso the social poet, and Pedroso the Chinese poet, and that the three, taken together, make up one solid Pedroso, a true and serious poet.

460. Vela, Arquelas. "Regino Pedroso y la recreación poética." *Teoría literaria del modernismo.* Mexico:

Ediciones Botas, 1950. Reprinted in *Bohemia*, no. 32 (August 7, 1970), 4-7.

Argues that Pedroso is the least subjective and the most lyrically pure poet of our time, one who has lived the experiences he writes about but who converts them into images and symbols.

See also Nos. 26, 62, 97, 100, 109, 157, 159, 160, 167, 173.

PRECIADO, ANTONIO (Ecuador)

A. Works

461. *Jolgorio*. Quito: Editorial Casa de la Cultura Ecuatoriana, 1961. 53pp.

462. *Tal como somos*. Quito: Ediciones Siglo XX, 1969.

Includes his composition "Siete veces la vida," which took first prize in a University Poetry Festival in 1967 in Ecuador.

B. Criticism

See Nos. 36, 121.

SANTA CRUZ, NICOMEDES (Peru, 1925-)

A. Works

463. *Décimas*. Lima: Editorial Juan Mejía Baca, 1959. 22pp.

A private edition not for commercial sale.

464. *Décimas*. Lima: Editorial Juan Mejía Baca, 1960. 146pp.

465. *Cumanana*. Lima: Editorial Juan Mejía Baca, 1964. 126pp.

466. *Canto a mi Perú*. Lima: Librería Studium, 1966.

467. *Décimas*. Lima: Librería Studium, 1966. 159pp.

468. *Décimas y poemas*. Lima: Campodónico Ediciones, 1971. 396pp.

Largely contains poems from his previous books but includes as well poetry not collected in book form, some dating back to 1949.

469. *Ritmos negros del Perú.* Buenos Aires: Losada, 1971. Reprint. 1973. 110pp.

B. Criticism

470. Alegría, Ciro. "El canto del pueblo." *El comercio* (July 22, 1960). Reprinted in Nicomedes Santa Cruz. *Décimas* (see No. 467), pp. 9-13.

Affirms that one of the most original and distinctive traits of Santa Cruz's poetry is his humor. Reviews several of his poetic themes, including the poet's nationalism.

471. Kattar, Jeannette. "Nicomedes Santa Cruz, poète noir de Pérou." *Annales de la faculté des Lettres et Sciences Humaines de Dakar*, no. 7 (1977), 183-208.

Calls Santa Cruz the best Afro-Peruvian poet at the present time. Sees his poetry, though inspired--like Nicolás Guillén's--by his ethnic background, as a useful contribution to understanding the culture and identity of the Peruvian people. Argues that his work belongs as well to Third World committed poetry.

472. Lafforgue, Jorge. "Prólogo." Nicomedes Santa Cruz. *Ritmos negros del Perú.* Buenos Aires: Losada, 1971. Reprint. 1973, pp. 7-10.

Emphasizes the popular nature of Santa Cruz's poetry and his place in the tradition of black poetry in the Americas.

473. Poniatowska, Elena. "Habla el peruano Nicomedes Santa Cruz." *¡Siempre!*, no. 1103 (August 14, 1974), 39-41, 70.

An interview in which the Peruvian poet charges Peru with cultural discrimination. In this interview Santa Cruz also defends Third World culture with its African, Asian, and Latin American roots against claims that its folkloric and popular nature is inferior to Western culture. Dismisses as garbage the belief that there is a distinction between popular and erudite poetry.

474. Richards, Henry J., and Teresa C. Salas. "Nicomedes
      Santa Cruz y la poesía de negritud." *Cuadernos ameri-*
      canos, 202 (1975), 182-199.

      Reviews the poet's publishing history. Places Santa
      Cruz within the Hispanic tradition of *decimistas* while
      discussing him as a poet of negritude whose work can be
      classified into such thematic categories as African
      cultural heritage, racial and social oppression, race
      pride, humor, and liberation.

See also Nos. 17, 118, 129, 154.

SOJO, JUAN PABLO   (Venezuela, 1908-1948)

      A. Works

475. *Tierras del Estado Miranda.*   Caracas: Artes Gráficos,
      1938. 56pp.

476. *Nochebuena negra.* Caracas: Editorial General Rafael
      Urdaneta, 1943. 182pp. 2nd ed. Caracas: Monte Avila
      Editores, 1972. 319pp.

477. *Temas y apuntes afro-venezolanos.* Caracas: Tip. La
      Nación, 1943. 60pp.

      B. Criticism

         1. Books

478. Lhaya, Pedro. *Juan Pablo Sojo, pasión y acento de su*
      tierra. Caracas: Instituto Nacional de Cultura y
      Bellas Artes, 1968. 157pp.

      Contends that Sojo's efforts opened the way to the
      scientific study of the Black in Venezuela. Asserts
      that Sojo's entire output shows the influence of his
      father, one of the first in Venezuela to take an inter-
      est in folklore. Argues that Sojo's work is imbued with
      the *magia* associated with the black world in which he
      lived and that became the focal point of his fiction,
      poetry, theater, and essays. Sees Sojo as a self-
      taught writer who learned more from his environment
      than from books, one whose development was cut short by
      an early death. Argues that Sojo was a lyrical and
      erotic writer, a folklorist whose objective was social
      protest. Characterizes Sojo as a writer of magic real-
      ism and social realism whose *Nochebuena negra* is poetic

in tone but weak in structure. Asserts that Sojo creates and maintains the erotic atmosphere in the novel with chapter titles, background descriptions, narrative scenes, and through such stylistic devices as humanization and what he calls *climatization*, where human qualities are described by pointing to things in the environment similar to them.

2. Articles, Shorter Studies, and Dissertations

479. Lhaya, Pedro. "El tema negro en la literatura venezolana." *Imagen*, no. 110 (1977), 34-38.

Lhaya argues that there was no black "Negritude movement" as such in Venezuelan literature but rather only some negristic influence, with Juan Pablo Sojo's *Nochebuena negra* the best and most authentic example of what there was. Includes two poems of Sojo's which he sees as the most authentic expressions of black poetry in Venezuela.

480. Liscano, Juan. "Prólogo." Juan Pablo Sojo. *Nochebuena negra*. 2nd ed. Caracas: Monte Avila Editores, 1972, pp. 7-11.

Argues that the authenticity of the novel in its treatment of the Barlovento region overshadows its stylistic and structural defects. Affirms that folklore is well integrated into the novel and is not an added extra. Believes that language use constitutes one of the principal merits of the novel, which mixes lyricism and sensuality.

481. Lubio Cardozo, Juan Pinto. "Sojo, Juan Pablo." *Diccionario general de la literatura venezolana (autores)*. Mérida, Venezuela: Centro de Investigaciones Literarias, Universidad de los Andes, 1974, pp. 725-729.

Surveys Sojo's brief but productive career, which included several unpublished works and one major unfinished volume. Lubio Cardoza contends that this volume would have placed Sojo in the front ranks of research specialists on the Black in America. Sees the influence of Nicolás Guillén on Sojo and concludes that the novelist was unhappy with Rómulo Gallegos' *Pobre negro*.

See also Nos. 12, 17, 21, 143, 165.

VALDES, GABRIEL DE LA CONCEPCION ("PLACIDO")   (Cuba, 1809-1844)

A. Works

482. *Poesías de Plácido.* Matanzas: Imprenta de Gobierno y Marina, 1838. 245pp.

483. *El veguero.* Matanzas: Imprenta de Comercio, 1841. 1842. 48pp.

484. *Poesías escogidas de Plácido.* Matanzas: Imprenta de Gobierno y Marina, 1842. 96pp.

485. *El hijo de maldición: poema del tiempo de las cruzadas.* Matanzas: Imprenta de Gobierno y Marina, 1843. 45pp.

486. *Poesías de Plácido.* Edited by Francisco Javier Vingut. New York: Roe, Lockwood and Son, 1854. 466pp. 2nd ed. 1855. 479pp. 3rd ed. 1956. 2 vols. 333pp., 324pp.

   The third edition is the most complete of the three. Contains one of the first attempts to outline the biographical facts of Plácido's life.

487. *Poesías completas de Plácido (Gabriel de la Concepción Valdés).* Paris: Editorial Española de Mme. C. Schmitz, 1857. 418pp. 2nd ed. 1862.

488. *Poesías completas.* Edited by Sebastián Alfredo de Morales. Havana: Librería y Efectos de Escritorio, 1886. 679pp. Buenos Aires: Casa Editorial Maucci Hermano, 1903. 391pp.

   Morales was a close friend of Plácido and his edition and biographical introduction draw on this close association. Usually considered to be the most reliable edition, even though the authenticity of some of the entries has been questioned.

489. *Poesías completas de Plácido.* Edited by Antonio María Eligio de la Puente. Havana: Editorial Cultural, 1930. 313pp.

   Contains an introductory biographical essay that includes a discussion of the merits and defects of Plácido's poetry. Concludes that there is very little in Plácido's verse to lead one to consider him a revolutionary poet.

490. *Los poemas más representativos de Plácido.* Edited by
      Frederick Stimson and Humberto Robles. Chapel Hill:
      Estudios de Hispanófila, 1976. 138pp.

      The most recent edition of Plácido's poetry. The
      modernized selections are based primarily on the Sebas-
      tián Alfredo de Morales edition of 1886 (see No. 488).
      Believing it impossible to organize Plácido's poetry
      chronologically, compilers group selections thematically.

B. Criticism

1. Bibliography

491. Cervantes, Carlos A. "Bibliografía Placidiana." *Re-
      vista cubana*, 8 (1937), 155-186.

      Updates Trelles' bibliography (see No. 492) by list-
      ing works on Plácido that appeared between 1904 and
      1937. Also includes Plácido's birth and death certifi-
      cates and other documentation and trivia associated
      with the poet together with poems dedicated to him.

492. Trelles, Carlos M. "Bibliografía placidiana." *Cuba y
      América* (July 3, 1904).

      Not seen but referred to by Carlos A. Cervantes as
      the bibliography for which he prepared his supplement
      (see No. 491). According to Cervantes, Trelles' bibliog-
      raphy listed Plácido's works, translations of his works,
      and studies about his life, his publications, and his
      death.

2. Books

493. Bar-Lewaw, Isaac. *Plácido.* Mexico: Ediciones Botas,
      1960. 183pp.

      One of the most recent studies of Plácido's life and
      work. Argues that Plácido because of his mild tempera-
      ment was not and could not have been guilty of a con-
      spiracy to exterminate Whites, that he was not aggres-
      sive enough to be a revolutionary, and that his revolu-
      tionary verse was mere theorizing. Contends further
      that Plácido's religious spirit led him to believe that
      compensation for his suffering would come in the after-
      life and not here on earth through armed struggle
      against tyranny. Also contends that Plácido's poetry,
      which he sees laced with biblical references, is very
      uneven in quality, although Plácido is one of Cuba's

most popular poets. Includes essential facts about
Plácido's life and work.

494. Casals, Jorge. *Plácido como poeta cubano.* Havana:
      Publicaciones del Ministerio de Educación, 1944.
      199pp.

      Casals' volume is largely a selected anthology of
      Plácido's poetry which contains as well a biographical
      sketch of the poet.

495. Figarola-Caneda, Domingo. *Plácido (poeta cubano).*
      Havana: El Siglo XX, 1922. 276pp.

      Begins his volume with twenty pages of differing re-
      actions to an alleged sketch of Plácido that was first
      brought to light on February 9, 1885. Gives a balanced
      review of the polemical history of Plácido complete
      with reproduction of important documents.

496. Garofalo Mesa, García. *Plácido, poeta y mártir.* Mexi-
      co: Ediciones Botas, 1944. 298pp.

      One of the first biographies of Plácido written in
      this century, but based on previously established ma-
      terial both legal and biographical. Charges that under
      government pressure the Cuban press in Plácido's time
      influenced the public against the poet by accusing him
      of conspiracy. Says that Plácido aspired to "true
      liberty."

497. Horrego Estuch, Leopoldo. *Plácido, el poeta infortunado.*
      Havana, 1944. 1949. 1960. 205pp.

      Updates earlier editions with new material in his
      1960 edition. Argues that Plácido dissimulated very
      well his desire for liberty but that the Spanish au-
      thorities were not deceived. Does not believe, however,
      that Plácido was head of a revolutionary movement.

498. Hostos, Eugenio María de. *Biografía de Plácido.* Santi-
      ago de Chile, 1872. Reprinted as "Plácido" in his
      Meditando. Paris: Sociedad de Ediciones Literarias
      y Artísticas, 1909, pp. 95-144. Reprinted in *Obras
      completas*, Vol. IX. Havana, 1939.

      Argues that Plácido was a martyr who was executed be-
      cause the Spanish authorities saw him as a threat to
      their control in the colonies. Contends also that the
      praises Plácido sang to the royal family and to the

Governor General of Cuba were false, a smokescreen to take suspicion off his plotting and cunning.

499. Laso de los Velez, Pedro. *Plácido, su biografía, juicio crítico, y análisis de sus más escogidas poesías.* Barcelona: Imprenta Barcelonesa, 1875.

500. Márquez, José de Jesús. *Plácido y los conspiradores de 1844.* Havana: La Constancia, 1894. 62pp.

Considered to be one of the most complete accounts of the *conspiración*. Argues that Cuban Blacks were inspired by black uprisings in Haiti. Contends as well that Plácido's argument was against white racists who enslaved Blacks and not against the crown and government.

501. Saiz de la Mora, Jesús. *Plácido, su popularidad, su obra, y sus críticos.* Havana: Aviador Comercial, 1919.

502. Stimson, Frederick S. *Cuba's Romantic Poet. The Study of Plácido.* Chapel Hill: University of North Carolina, 1964. 150pp.

Discusses all of the aspects of the story of Plácido. Uses published sources but draws as well on additional unpublished information from the New York Public Library, the Harvard University Library, and libraries in Cuba. Also discusses the fictionalized biographies never before considered in Plácido studies. Provides a background sketch of the Caribbean in Plácido's time, seen from a North American perspective in that it draws on the "impressions" recorded by many visitors from the United States to the Island of Plácido's day. Argues that too much emphasis has been put on the sensational aspects of Plácido's story, especially by North American critics; that Plácido's fame should rest more on his aesthetics than on his heroics; and that in any event, he did not have the temperament to have been the conspirator some think he was.

3. Articles, Shorter Studies, and Dissertations

503. Bachiller y Morales, Antonio. "Plácido." *Revista cubana*, 2 (1885), 547-561.

Sets out to prove Plácido innocent of involvement in the conspiracy.

504. Bernal, Emilia. "Los poetas mártires, Gabriel de la
      Concepción Valdés: su vida y su obra." *Cuba contempo-*
      ránea, 35 (1924), 216-232.

      Argues that the legendary side of Plácido's biography
      has exaggerated and distorted the truth. Contends that
      the criticism has erred in every extreme. Calls Plácido
      an "immortal bastard" and ranks him with Poe, Verlaine,
      and Darío. Affirms that Plácido's best work was con-
      tained in his first published book of poetry in 1839
      and that subsequent published work was of a quality that
      only tarnished his reputation.

505. Carruthers, Ben Frederic. "The Life, Work and Death of
      Plácido." Ph.D. dissertation, University of Illinois,
      1941. 262pp.

      An early attempt to give Plácido the attention in
      English Carruthers thought he deserved. Argues that
      any study of black contributions to Cuban poetry must
      begin with Plácido. Reviews Plácido's life, which he
      divides into the following periods: 1809-1834, 1834-
      1840, 1840-1842, and 1842-1844. Offers a critique of
      Plácido's poetry which he classifies as love poetry,
      elegiac poetry, narrative poetry, patriotic poetry,
      poetry of occasion, didactic and religious poetry. Con-
      cludes by comparing Plácido in racial heritage to Alex-
      andre Dumas père and to Alexander Pushkin. Includes in
      an appendix Plácido's will, death certificate, a trans-
      lation of "La fatalidad," and a letter from Prof. Elías
      Entralgo, holder of the Chair of Cuban History, Uni-
      versity of Havana, who asserted that Plácido did not
      have the temperament to get involved in insurrection.

506. Castellanos, Jorge. "Plácido, poeta social." *Exilio.*
      Revista de las humanidades, 5 (1971), 63-96.

      Argues that Plácido the romantic poet and Plácido the
      victim of a corrupt and tyrannical political system
      should also be seen as a poet-observer of Cuban society,
      1834-1844, as this side of his work has been overlooked.
      A close study of Plácido's poetry reveals, he contends,
      strong social responsibility and a sustained process of
      growth in his development that his biographers have not
      noted.

507. ———. "Plácido, ¿víctima o mártir?" *Exilio. Revista*
      de las humanidades, 7 (1973), 31-48.

Determines that Plácido was either a victim of a plot by the Spanish authorities and the slave owners or a martyr conscious of what he was doing for two causes, namely, freedom of the slaves and independence for the country. Concludes that Plácido was both victim and martyr and that he unofficially aided those causes, which makes the official charges against him unjust, even though in his poetry he consciously declared himself opposed to tyranny.

508. Cobb, Martha K. "Plácido: the Poet-Hero." *Negro History Bulletin*, 38 (1975), 374-375.

A brief account of Plácido's heroic life, with an English translation of the poem "Despedida a mi madre," which Plácido wrote in the Chapel of the Hospital de Santa Cristina on the night of his execution.

509. Durán Rosado, Esteban. "Plácido, poeta popular cubano." *Revista mexicana de cultura*. Supl. *El nacional*, no. 1091 (1968), 3.

Contends from the outset that Plácido was not one of the great poets of nineteenth-century Cuba. Holds to the view that the poet was an uneducated spontaneous versifier but one who was so popular that people learned some of his work by heart, particularly after his execution. Durán Rosado argues also that Plácido was not the conspirator he was accused of being.

510. Franco, José L. "Plácido: una polémica que tiene cien años." *Plácido y otros ensayos*. Havana: Ediciones Unión, 1964, pp. 7-20.

Reviews in chronological order many of the major statements made during the second half of the nineteenth century about the life and works of Plácido, with illustrative quotations from critical works mentioned. Opinions surveyed range from Francisco Calcagno's assertion of Plácido's guilt--more to his heroic credit than a plea of innocence--to the retort of Cirilo Villaverde who saw the poet as the white man's friend.

511. González-Cruz, Luis F. "El romanticismo cubano: algunas precisiones." *Caribe*, 1 (1976), 87-99.

Emphasizes Plácido's "Indianist" verse, his love poetry, and his poetry on nature. Believes his heroic poems are too far removed from Cuban reality.

512. González del Valle, Francisco. "¿Es de Plácido 'La
      plegaria a Dios'?" *Cuba contemporánea*, 33 (1923),
      127-160, 232-274.

      Discusses the religious tone of the poem and its
      metrics. Points out that Plácido proclaims his inno-
      cence in this poem, in his "Adios a mi lira," in his
      "Despedida a mi madre," and in his will.

513. Leavitt, Sturgis E. "Latin-American Literature in the
      United States." *Revue de Littérature Comparée*, 11
      (1931), 126-148.

      Focuses on Plácido's popularity in the United States.
      Writes that Dr. Wurdeman in his *Notes on Cuba* (Boston,
      1844) was the first in this country to mention the
      Cuban poet. Quotes from Wurdeman who wrote that "at
      the head of ... [a conspiracy] was a mulatto poet of
      Matanzas, Gabriel de la Concepción Valdés, whose verses,
      under the signature of Plácido, had often been admitted
      into the daily journals" (p. 355). Reviews Wurdeman's
      work including his scrapbook (now at Harvard) which
      contains a number of Plácido's poems.

514. Menéndez Pelayo, Marcelino. "Cuba." *Historia de la
      poesía hispanoamericana*. Madrid: Consejo Superior de
      Investigaciones Científicas, 1948, pp. 209-286.

      Contains Menéndez Pelayo's well-known assertion, first
      made in 1893, that Plácido's fame can rest on the quali-
      ty of certain poems (the majority of Plácido's poems he
      thought should be burned) and not on the fact that he
      was a Mulatto executed for his political involvement.

515. Mitjans, Aurelio. "La poesía lírica." *Estudio sobre
      el movimiento científico y literario de Cuba*. Havana:
      A. Alvarez y Cía., 1890. Reprint. Havana: Consejo
      Nacional de Cultura, 1963, pp. 147-156.

      Extremely critical of Plácido's poetic technique,
      which, he says, the poet was unable to develop, owing
      to difficult circumstances. Says that it is difficult
      to conjecture whether given better circumstances Plácido
      would have been a better poet, for example, than Heredia.
      Contends that Plácido wrote incorrect verse that was
      careless in form and pedestrian in theme. Dismisses as
      pure fantasy some of the laudatory comments on Plácido's
      poetry.

516. Osiek, Betty Tyree. "Plácido: Critic of the Vice-Ridden Masters and of the Abuses of the Enslaved Black." *SECOLAS Annals* (Southern Conference on Latin American Studies), 9 (1978), 62-67.

Sees hatred of tyranny and oppression as one of the main themes in Plácido's poetry. Contends that Plácido expressed his ideas about the ruling forces in society in his fables and other poems and that he was skilled in the art of doubletalk, for example, by writing about injustices elsewhere when he meant Cuba.

517. Piñeyro, Enrique. "Gabriel de la Concepción Valdés 'Plácido.'" *Biografías americanas*. Paris: Garnier Hermanos, 1906, pp. 329-359.

Observes that Plácido's reputation has passed through two different periods, one of excessive praise and one of excessive criticism. Gives valuable insights into Plácido's life and work. Recognizes serious defects in Placido's poetic diction but asserts that these could have been overcome had the poet enjoyed better opportunities to develop his craft.

518. Rivera, Guillermo. "El ensayo de Hostos sobre Plácido." *Hispania*, 22 (1939), 145-152.

Points out that Hostos' essay on Plácido, written in 1877, has appeared in several subsequent volumes of the author's work but always in a shortened form and with variants.

519. Sanguily, Manuel. "Un improvisador cubano." *Hojas literarias*, 3 (1894), 93-121.

Attacks Plácido on every front.

520. ———. "Otra vez Plácido y Menéndez Pelayo." *Hojas literarias*, 3 (1894), 227-269.

Continues to attack Plácido on every front.

521. Torriente, Lola de la. "Plácido, un poeta víctima del prejuicio racial." *Bohemia*, no. 15 (June 24, 1966), 100-102, 113.

Largely a biographical review that covers the poet's life and the political background of his time.

522. Vitier, Cintio. "Cubanía de Plácido." *Lo cubano en la poesía*. Havana: Instituto del Libro, 1970, pp. 90-101.

Does not take Plácido's revolutionary verse seriously.
Argues that his "El juramento" is more rhetoric than
reality.

See also Nos. 25, 28, 37, 52, 64, 79, 85, 95, 98, 100, 101,
111, 117, 122, 123, 125, 133, 149, 153, 160, 161, 166, 170,
171, 173, 174, 183.

VALDES, JOSE MANUEL   (Peru, 1767-1844)

A. Works

523. *Salterio peruano o paráfrasis de los ciento cincuenta
      salmos de David, y algunos cánticos sagrados, en verso
      castellano, para instrucción y piadoso ejercicio de
      todos los fieles, y principalmente de los peruanos.*
      Lima: J. Masías, 1833. 472pp. Reprint. 1863.

524. *Poesías espirituales escritas a beneficio y para el uso
      de las personas sensibles y piadosas.* n.p., 1836.
      96pp.

525. *Vida admirable del bienaventurado Fr. Martín de Porres,
      natural de Lima y donado profeso en el convento del
      Rosario del Orden de Predicadores de esta ciudad.*
      Lima: J. Masías, 1840. 192pp. Reprint. 1863.

B. Criticism

526. King, Anita. "José Valdés." *Essence* (February, 1977),
      30.

      A brief review of the life and hardships of José
      Manuel Valdés with emphasis on his medical and profes-
      sional accomplishments.

527. Romero, Fernando. "José Manuel Valdés, gran mulato del
      Perú." *Revista bimestre cubana*, 43 (1939), 178-209.
      Translated by Mercer Cook as "José Manuel Valdés,
      Great Peruvian Mulatto." *Phylon*, 3 (1942), 297-319.

      The major study available to date on José Manuel
      Valdés. Includes a bibliography of the poet that con-
      tains a list of his professional and medical works and
      a bibliography of works about him. Argues that Valdés
      was the first Black in the New World to achieve a high
      social position, but that he wrote "white" verse, like
      Manzano and Plácido. Compares his poetry to Plácido's

and concludes that Plácido was a popular poet and Valdés an academic one.

VASCONCELOS, JOSE ("El Negrito Poeta") (Mexico, 1722?-1760?)

A. Works

528. León, Nicolás. *El Negrito Poeta Mexicano y sus populares versos*. Mexico: Imprenta del Museo Nacional, 1912. 234pp. Reprint. Culiacán: Ediciones del Gobierno del Estado de Sinaloa, 1961. 141pp.

Compiles from private archives an edition of the "Calendario del Negrito Poeta," first published by Simón Blanquel between 1856 and 1869. Gives what little biographical information about El Negrito Poeta that is available, namely, that he was born in Almolonga between 1722 and 1734, that his parents were from the Congo, that it is not known whether he ever learned to read or how he managed to free himself from slavery. States also that Fernández de Lizardi mentions him in his *El Periquillo Sarniento* and that he must have died around 1760. Publishes and comments on the poet's *coplas*.

B. Criticism

529. Campos, Rubén M. "La tradición del Negrito Poeta." *El folklore literario de México*. Mexico: Publicaciones de la Secretaria de Educación Pública, 1929, pp. 85-104.

Contends that El Negrito Poeta for two hundred years has personified "people's humor" in Mexico. Affirms that verse wrongly attributed to him can be determined easily because it lacks the ingenuity, wit, and humor of his authentic improvisations. Considers El Negrito Poeta--as a representative of an oppressed people--to be an authentic precursor of the rebellious spirit that led to Mexican independence.

530. Higuera, Gral. Ernesto. "Reseña apologética." Nicolás León. *El Negrito Poeta Mexicano y sus populares versos*. 1961, pp. 5-6.

Considers "the famous Little Black Poet" to be one of the outstanding figures of Colonial Mexico. Argues that he was one of the first to feel the need for Mexico to become an independent nation. Contends that in the verse of this "great improviser" we can see much refer-

ence to the political and economic exploitation of the
Mexican people. Argues that in this regard El Negrito
Poeta had much in common with Fernández de Lizardi and
with Sor Juana Inés de la Cruz.

531. Mendoza, Vicente T. "Algo del folklore negro en México."
      Miscelánea en homenaje a Fernandez Ortiz. Havana:
      Ucar y García y Cía., 1955. Vol. I, pp. 1095-1111.

      Contends that El Negrito Poeta got on well with every-
      body as he, in a sense, associated with all kinds, in-
      cluding viceroys, from one end of Mexico to the other.
      Argues that details of the popular poet's life can be
      found in his verse. Affirms that Vasconcelos was a
      pure Black but one who was, at the same time, pure Mexi-
      can.

532. Torre, Manuel. "La poesía y la danza de los negros en
      México." *El nacional* (August 13, 1944), 3.

      Argues that the black influence in Mexican poetry,
      music, and dance is very important. Affirms that this
      influence is important not only for determining imported
      ethnic characteristics but also for its historical,
      linguistic, poetic, and choreographic matters as well.
      Contends that the Negrito Poeta, "who rubbed shoulders
      with viceroys, bishops, and nobles," can serve as a
      typical example, a point of departure.

WILSON, CARLOS GUILLERMO ("CUBENA") (Panama, 1941-)

      A. Works

533. *Cuentos del negro Cubena.* Guatemala: Editorial Landívar,
      1977. 94pp.

534. *Pensamientos del negro Cubena.* Los Angeles, 1977. 48pp.

      Cubena's first collection of poetry.

      B. Criticism

535. Alvarado, Juan. "Caída y resurrección." *Vida*, 5
      (1977), 3-4.

      Studies Cubena's poetry and finds that his *Pensamientos
      del negro Cubena* complements very well his short stories
      as in both genres he calls attention to racism, expresses
      a commitment to justice, and reveals an intense love for
      humanity.

536. Mercurius, Jeanette. *"Cuentos del negro Cubena*: A Review."* Modern Language Review* (Georgetown, Guyana) (December 1977-January 1978), 84-89.

Writes that Cubena's collection of twelve short stories "brings to light the contemporary Panamanian socio-political situation as seen from the point of view of a member of the group representative of the underdogs in Panamanian society, namely, the Negroes." Asserts that Cubena writes in the tradition of the realist and naturalist schools of French and Hispanic literature but with some new novelistic techniques. Divides Cubena's short stories into three main categories, stories dealing with (1) racial prejudice in Panama, (2) black protest, and (3) attitudes of white North Americans toward Blacks. Concludes that Cubena has faith that the Black will achieve his rightful place in society.

536a. Smart, Ian. "Big Rage and Big Business." *Caribbean Review.* In press.

Analyzes Cubena's *tremendista* prose and his experimental poetry. Examines influences and argues that black Latin American literature has come of age in this century. Concludes that Cubena's work is an artistic expression of intense outrage.

537. ————. "The *tremendismo negrista* in *Cuentos del negro Cubena."* Studies in Afro-Hispanic Literature.* Vol. II. Edited by Clementine Rabassa and Gladys Seda-Rodríguez. Forthcoming.

Uses Adalberto Ortiz's characterization of Cubena's stories as *tremendismo negrista* to illustrate what Smart agrees is their fundamental trait. Examines the stylistic devices Wilson uses to achieve his aesthetic objectives. Concludes that in his stories we can find strong endings, suspense, and truncated narrative to help create the *tremendista* effect. Argues that Cubena's themes are chosen largely to illustrate the more vicious aspects of the white man's racism and inhumanity. Smart also relates Cubena's work to the realism of Caribbean "yard" literature.

ZAPATA OLIVELLA, JUAN   (Colombia, 1922–   )

A. Works

538. *Albedrío total*. Guatemala, 1970.

539. *La bruja de portezuela (drama)*. Bogotá: Instituto
     Colombiano de Cultura, 1972. 70pp.

540. *Panecea. Poesía liberada*. Cartagena: Editora Bolívar,
     1976. 136pp.

B. Criticism

See No. 118.

ZAPATA OLIVELLA, MANUEL   (Colombia, 1920–   )

A. Works

541. *Tierra mojada*. Bogotá: Editorial Espiral, 1947. Madrid:
     Editorial Bullón, 1964. 315pp.

542. *Pasión vagabunda (relatos)*. Bogotá: Editorial Santa Fe,
     1949. 234pp.

543. *He visto la noche (relatos)*. Bogotá: Editorial Andes,
     1953. Medellín: Editorial Bedout, 1969, 1974. 182pp.

544. *Hotel de vagabundos (drama)*. Bogotá: Editorial Espiral,
     1955

545. *China 6 A.M. (relatos)*. Bogotá: Editorial S.S.B., 1957.

546. *La calle 10*. Bogotá: Ediciones Casa de la Cultura,
     1960. 126pp.

547. *Corral de negros*. Havana: Casa de las Américas, 1963.
     230pp.

     Published in Medellín by Editorial Bedout in 1966 and
     1974 with a new title, *Chambacú, corral de negros*.

548. *Detrás del rostro*. Madrid: Ediciones Aguilar, 1963.
     160pp.

549. *En Chimá nace un santo*. Barcelona: Editorial Seix Barral,
     1963. 160pp.

550. *Cuentos de muerte y libertad.* Bogotá: Editorial
Iqueima, 1965.

551. *¿Quién dió el fusil a Oswald? (cuentos).* Bogotá:
Editorial Revista Colombiana, 1967. 87pp.

552. *Caronte liberado (drama).* Bogotá: Instituto Colombiano
de Cultura, 1972. 35pp.

553. *El hombre colombiano.* Bogotá: Colección Enciclopedia
de los Fundadores, 1974. 401pp.

Perhaps Zapata Olivella's most important nonliterary
work.

B. Criticism

554. Alegría, Ciro. "Prólogo." Manuel Zapata Olivella.
Tierra mojada. Editorial Bullón, 1964, pp. 1-14.

Writes that Zapata Olivella sees his characters "from
within" but that this closeness is converted into propaganda. Considers Zapata Olivella to be one of the first
black novelists in Spanish America.

555. Anillo Sarmiento, Antonio. "La novelística comprometida
de Manuel Zapata Olivella." Ph.D. dissertation,
George Washington University, 1972. 280pp.

Approaches his subject by focusing on the man, his
work, and his social milieu. Believes Zapata Olivella
shares the *americanismo* of Bello, the *mesianismo* of
Martí, and the pedogogical character of Hostos. Considers one of the big defects of his novels to be the
inconclusive endings, that is, the uncertainty surrounding the destiny of some of the characters. Affirms
that *Chambacú, corral de negros* is Zapata Olivella's
most important novel, one in which the author writes
in the service of Blacks.

556. Botero, Ebel. "Manuel Zapata Olivella. *¿Quién dió el
fusil a Oswald?*" *20 escritores contemporáneos.*
Manizales: Tipografía Arbelaez, 1969, pp. 160-169.

Affirms that social themes dominate Zapata Olivella's
narrative, an outgrowth of his obsession for social
justice. Racial discrimination both in the United
States and in Colombia are the specific problems that
most concern him as the stories in this collection for
the most part deal with black problems. Contends that

Zapata Olivella's ideological zeal does not cloud his thorough grounding in modern artistic techniques.

557. Doerr, Richard Paul. "La magia como dinámica de evasión en la novelística de Manuel Zapata Olivella." Ph.D. dissertation, University of Colorado, 1973. 239pp.

Argues that Zapata Olivella's prime concerns in his literature include the folklore, beliefs, and practices of Colombia's mestizo, mulatto, and black population, whose dependency on "magic" provides the only answer to many of their pressing problems. The works that best illustrate this "magical reaffirmation" of his people are *Tierra mojada*, *Chambacú*, *corral de negros*, and *En Chimá nace un santo*.

558. Kooreman, Thomas E. "Two Novelists' Views of the Bogotazo." *Latin American Literary Review*, 3 (1974), 131–135.

Places Zapata Olivella in the Latin American novelistic tradition of social protest. Considers his *La Calle 10* to be an artistic treatment of the *bogotazo* manifestation of *la violencia*.

559. Ruiz Camacho, Rubén. "*Detrás del rostro*, una novela ejemplar." *Boletín cultural y bibliográfico*, 8 (1965), 105–106.

Considers *Detrás del rostro* to be one of the best Colombian novels of *la violencia*. Argues that Zapata Olivella's medical background helps make this work unique.

560. Ruiz Gómez, Darío. "La crítica como beligerencia verbal." *Letras nacionales*, no. 12 (1967), 17–24.

Includes Manuel Zapata Olivella among what he believes can be called a generation of 1950 or a generation of *la violencia* in Colombia.

561. Sohn, Guansu. "La novela colombiana de protesta social." Ph.D. dissertation, University of Oklahoma, 1976. 169pp.

Contends that Manuel Zapata Olivella is a revolutionary in temperament but not a leftist ideologically. Sees his *Tierra mojada*, with its social protest theme, as having been influenced by Ciro Alegría's novel *El mundo es ancho y ajeno*. Agrees also that Arnoldo Palacios' novel *Las estrellas son negras* is a first-rate naturalistic novel.

562. Suárez Rondón, Gerardo. "Síntesis temática de la novela de violencia." *La novela sobre la violencia en Colombia*. Bogotá: Editor, Dr. Luis E. Serrano A., 1966, pp. 11-44.

Discusses *La calle 10* and *Detrás del rostro*. The former, he affirms, shows that rebellion without direction is doomed to failure. Considers *Detrás del rostro* one of the most interesting and important of the Colombian novels of violence.

See also Nos. 12, 17, 65, 76, 94, 103, 118, 143, 145, 146, 162.

APPENDIX:

PERIODICALS CITED

Acta literaria (Budapest)
African Forum (New York)
América indígena (Mexico)
American Hispanist (Clear
  Creek, Ind.)
Américas (Washington, D.C.)
Archivos del folklore cubano
  (Havana)
Atenea (Concepción)
Atlántida (Buenos Aires)
Biblioteca Nacional José
  Martí (Havana)
Black Scholar (Sausalito,
  Cal.)
Black Sociologist (Princeton,
  N.J.)
Black World (Chicago)
Bohemia (Havana)
Boletín cultural y biblio-
  gráfico (Bogotá)
Bulletin hispanique (Bordeaux)
Caribbean Quarterly (Kingston,
  Jamaica)
Caribbean Review (Miami)
Caribbean Studies (Rio
  Piedras)
Caribe (Honolulu)
Carteles (Havana)
Casa de las Américas (Havana)
Center for Cuban Studies
  Newsletter (New York)
College Language Association
  Journal (Baltimore)
Comercio (Lima)
Comercio (Quito)

Comparative Literature
  Studies (Urbana, Ill.)
Cuadernos (Paris)
Cuadernos americanos (Mexico)
Cuadernos de filología
  (Valparaiso)
Cuadernos hispanoamericanos
  (Madrid)
Cuba internacional (Havana)
Cuba y América (Havana)
Daedalus (Boston)
De la prensa internacional
  (Havana)
Diario de Panamá (Panama)
Diario del Caribe (Barran-
  quilla)
Elite (Caracas)
Essence (New York)
Estudios afrocubanos
  (Havana)
Estudios americanos (Sevilla)
Etnología y folklore (Havana)
Exilio. Revista de las
  humanidades (New York)
Expresiones culturales del
  Ecuador (Quito)
El farol (Caracas)
Freedomways (New York)
La gaceta de Cuba (Havana)
Hispania (Stanford)
Hojas literarias (Havana)
Hoy (Havana)
Humanitas (Tucumán)
Humanitas. Boletín ecuatori-
  ana de antropología (Quito)

Imagen (Caracas)
Inter-American Review of Bibliography (Revista interamericana de bibliografía) (Washington, D.C.)
Jamaican Journal (Kingston, Jamaica)
Journal of Negro History (Washington, D.C.)
Kentucky Romance Quarterly (Lexington)
Latin American Literary Review (Pittsburgh)
Latin American Research Review (Chapel Hill, N.C.)
Letras del Ecuador (Quito)
Letras nacionales (Bogotá)
Lotería (Panamá)
Mercurio peruano (Lima)
Modern Language Review (Georgetown, Guyana)
Montalbán (Caracas)
Mundo (San Juan)
Mundo nuevo (París)
Nacional (Mexico)
Negro History Bulletin (Washington, D.C.)
Norte (Amsterdam)
Norte/Sur. Canadian Journal of Latin American Studies (Vancouver)
Nosotros (Buenos Aires)
Nuestra raza (Montevideo)
Nueva revista cubana (Havana)
Parnassus. Poetry in Review (New York)
Phylon (Atlanta)
Présence Africaine (Paris)
Razón y fábula (Bogotá)
Revista América (Havana)
Revista bimestre cubana (Havana)
Revista chicano-riqueña (Gary, Ind.)
Revista crisol (México)
Revista Cuba contemporánea (Havana)
Revista cubana (Havana)
Revista de América (Bogotá)

Revista de bellas artes (Mexico)
Revista de la biblioteca nacional de Cuba. Segundo serie (Havana)
Revista de la Universidad de México (Mexico)
Revista de la Universidad de Yucatán (Yucatán)
Revista del pacífico (Valparaiso)
Revista iberoamericana (Pittsburgh)
Revista iberoamericana de literatura (Montevideo)
Revista mexicana de cultura (Mexico)
Revista nacional de cultura (Caracas)
Revista/Review Interamericana (Hato Rey, P.R.)
Révue de Littérature Comparée (Paris)
The Rican: A Journal of Contemporary Puerto Rican Thought (Chicago)
Saber vivir (Buenos Aires)
Santiago (Santiago)
SECOLAS Annals (Southeastern Conference on Latin American Studies)
¡Siempre! (México)
Sin nombre (San Juan, P.R.)
South Atlantic Bulletin (Chapel Hill, N.C.)
Sustancia (Tucumán)
Thesaurus (Bogotá)
Torre (Rio Piedras)
Ufahamu: Journal of the African activist association (Los Angeles)
Ultima hora (Havana)
Unión (Havana)
Universidad de Antioquia (Medellín)
Universidad de la Habana (Havana)
University of Toronto Quarterly (Toronto)
Vida (Los Angeles)

INDEX OF CRITICS

(Numbers refer to entries, not pages)